The Spoils

Also by Jesse Eisenberg

The Revisionist: A Play

Asuncion: A Play

The Spoils

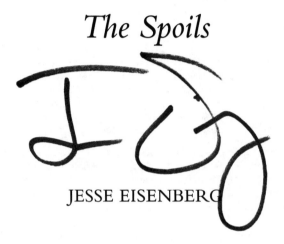

JESSE EISENBERG

Grove Press
New York

Published simultaneously in Canada
Printed in the United States of America

FIRST EDITION

ISBN 978-0-8021-2390-9
eISBN 978-0-8021-9139-7

Grove Press
an imprint of Grove Atlantic
154 West 14th Street
New York, NY 10011

Distributed by Publishers Group West

groveatlantic.com

15 16 17 18   10 9 8 7 6 5 4 3 2 1

The Spoils

PRODUCTION CREDITS

The Spoils was originally produced by The New Group (Scott Elliott, Artistic Director; Adam Bernstein, Executive Director) in association with Lisa Matlin, opening on June 2, 2015, at The Pershing Square Signature Center in New York City. It was directed by Scott Elliott; Set Design: Derek McLane; Costume Design: Susan Hilferty; Lighting Design: Peter Kaczorowski; Sound Design: Rob Milburn and Michael Bodeen; Projection Design: Olivia Sebesky; Fight Direction: Unkle-Dave's Fight-House; Production Supervisor: PRF Productions; Production Stage Manager: Valerie A. Peterson; Casting: Judy Henderson, CSA; Public Relations: Bridget Klapinski; Advertising: AKA; Associate Artistic Director: Ian Morgan; Development Director: Jamie Lehrer; General Management: DR Theatrical Management.

The cast was as follows:

Kalyan	Kunal Nayyar
Reshma	Annapurna Sriram
Ben	Jesse Eisenberg
Ted	Michael Zegen
Sarah	Erin Darke

CHARACTERS

KALYAN   Originally from Nepal, now in New York studying for an MBA. Ben's roommate.

RESHMA   Of Indian heritage but culturally American, now in medical school. Kalyan's girlfriend.

BEN   A young, angry man, in film school. Owns the apartment where he and Kalyan live.

TED   Ben's classmate from high school, now working on Wall Street.

SARAH   Ben's high school crush, now Ted's girlfriend.

•

"Know something about something. Don't just present your wonderful self to the world. Constantly amass knowledge and offer it around."—Richard Holbrooke, 22nd United States Ambassador to the United Nations

ACT 1

A PowerPoint presentation is illuminated on a white wall. The slide says:

Amusement or Barbarism?

Lights up on a modern apartment in New York City and a young Nepalese man, KALYAN, and his Indian girlfriend RESHMA. He speaks with an accent; she does not.

KALYAN   "Amusement or Barbarism?"

RESHMA   Am I supposed to choose one?

KALYAN   No, it's just a provocative opener.

RESHMA   Oh sorry.

KALYAN   That's okay. "Amusement or Barbarism?"

Kalyan hits a button on his laptop and the slide changes to:

American Football:
An Introduction to the Ballet of Brutality.
By Kalyan Mathema

KALYAN   "American Football: An Introduction to the Ballet of Brutality. By Kalyan Mathema." Now, before I continue, I must confess that I'm of two minds on this. I feel, in a truly legitimate way, torn. And it raises large questions about morality and ethics. Questions that all the great minds have tried to tackle. Pun intended. Did you see that? What I did with "tackle?" You'll notice that I have several puns sprinkled throughout this PowerPoint presentation.

5

RESHMA Oh god, lucky me!

KALYAN Continuing on. It raises a big question: Is it appropriate to withhold knowledge from someone even if you think it might hurt them? Is it ethical to deny someone information, even if disclosing that information might hurt them?

RESHMA Are you saying that telling me something, presumably scintillating, about football will hurt me?

KALYAN Well, I think it might hurt *us.*

RESHMA And how, exactly, will me knowing about football hurt us?

KALYAN Every Monday night, you and I gather together in this living room to watch NFL on ESPN, which is one of the great highlights of my week. In fact, it is the only highlight of my week. Is that too needy?

RESHMA It's a little needy. But I know it's the highlight and I appreciate your honesty.

KALYAN Thank you. And one of the things that makes it the highlight of my week—a week that's mostly spent reading economics textbooks and World Bank reports and fighting with my roommate—is that you don't know what's going on during the game. If I can speak frankly, I think it's so lovely that you don't know what anyone's doing on the field and yet you continue to come here, week after week, and let me put my arm around you while we watch something that I enjoy immensely and you simply tolerate.

RESHMA So what you're saying is, you think my ignorance is lovely?

KALYAN Amongst other things, very much so.

RESHMA I've heard pretty much every cheesy pickup line. And, usually, I'm complimented on my brilliance. But, Kalyan, never has someone been so sweet and insulted me at the same time. What else do you like about me?

6

KALYAN   I like it very much when you ask me why the blue team doesn't just kick it between the yellow things and I get to tell you that they're way too far away to kick a field goal.

RESHMA   What else?

KALYAN   I like it also when you ask me why thirty seconds is taking twenty minutes. I find that to be very charming, especially when it's followed by a sigh of frustration because you have to be up very early in the morning to save the lives of strangers at your hospital.

RESHMA   Anything else? Not football related?

KALYAN   If you're asking me to tell you what I like about you that's not football related, I'm afraid you will definitely not make it back in time to save any lives. Reshma, I like everything about you and all of the little things that you hide from other people, like that little protrusion near your elbow that you unconsciously cover with long sleeve shirts in the summer and the tooth that kind of turns inward and makes you talk with your mouth a little more closed than would be expected from someone with your verbal prowess. These are the things I like the most. I would like to buy you longer sleeves and braces but I would miss your elbow and tooth so much.

RESHMA   You are the sweetest person in the world. Do you know that?

KALYAN   I've only just been alerted.

RESHMA   You really are. You are the kindest, nicest guy. And I don't deserve you.

KALYAN   Don't say that.

RESHMA   No, really. I don't deserve you.

KALYAN   Of course you deserve me. The only reason you wouldn't deserve me is because you're so overqualified. So you wouldn't deserve me through some reverse logic.

RESHMA   Sweet comments like that are just another reason why I don't deserve you.

KALYAN   What does that mean?

RESHMA   Nothing, it means nothing. Just continue on with the PowerPoint.

KALYAN   Okay. "American Football: An Introduction to the Ballet of Brutality. By Kalyan Mathema."

Kalyan presses a button. The slide changes to read:

A Brief History: Bravery and Brevity

KALYAN   "A Brief History: Bravery and Brevity!"

RESHMA   Is that also a pun?

KALYAN   I think it's more a play on words.

RESHMA   'Cause now I'm just looking for puns.

KALYAN   And you'll find them.

Kalyan presses a button and there is a cheesy transition to a slide that says:

Rules and Regulations

KALYAN   "Rules and Regulations:"

And another slide:

Skin that Pig and Toss it on The Gridiron

KALYAN   "Skin that Pig and Toss it on The Gridiron."

RESHMA   I think that's a pun, but I don't understand the reference.

KALYAN   Don't worry, there are more on the way!

The door swings open and BEN *enters carrying groceries and a camera bag.*

BEN   Namaste, motherfuckers!

KALYAN Ben, what are you doing here?

BEN What am I doing in my own fucking home? Hey Reshma! You're looking very Indian tonight.

RESHMA Thanks Ben, you're looking smarmy.

BEN Was he doing a PowerPoint presentation for you? Were you doing a PowerPoint presentation for her?

KALYAN Ben, you said you would be at the bar for a while, you said this would be okay.

BEN This guy *loves* fucking PowerPoint! Any excuse to make a PowerPoint presentation. Someone asks him a question, a simple fucking query and he's off and running. Hey Kalyan, how was your day? Hold on a second, let me answer that via PowerPoint. Hey sir, do you have the time? I do, let me show you on some PowerPoint slides. Do I have something hanging out of my fucking nose? Well, I can answer that using seven different shitty graphics with clip art and transitions!

RESHMA Okay, we get it! He likes PowerPoint. I happen to think it's really sweet.

BEN Fine, but he's teaching you about football? How is that sweet? You don't wanna watch that brutal, barbaric shit, do you Reshma? You're a classy woman.

RESHMA And yet, when you say that, Ben, I somehow feel less classy.

BEN The world is topsy-turvy! You can't actually like football. Bunty only likes it because it makes him feel more American and less Nepalese, isn't that right Bunty?

KALYAN I'm sorry about this Reshma. Ben did tell me he was going to be out all night.

BEN Do you want me to head back out?

RESHMA No, you stay! I was just about to leave.

KALYAN   No you weren't. No, she wasn't.

BEN   Are you sure you want to leave? I don't want to break up the promising date you guys were probably having!

RESHMA   Well, if you have somewhere to go . . .

BEN   Really don't.

RESHMA   Why don't we just call it a night, and I'll call you tomorrow, Kalyan.

BEN   That does sound like the better idea, you're so smart all the time! Have a good night Reshie. Good to see you, as usual.

Reshma starts packing up her purse. Ben opens the door for her but stands in front of it.

BEN   Before you go . . .

RESHMA   Yes?

KALYAN   Ben . . .

BEN   Tell me you're the luckiest girl in the world.

RESHMA   What?

BEN   You are dating this fucking prince charming! This guy is my roommate and my best fucking friend in the world forever and if anyone does anything to hurt him or to touch him where he doesn't want to be touched or break his heart or even think of breaking that adorable fucking heart, I will personally track you down and slaughter you and enjoy it. So tell me you're the luckiest girl in the world.

RESHMA   Fuck you, Ben.

BEN   And give him a little kiss so he knows you appreciate him.

KALYAN   Ben, I don't need help.

BEN   Clearly you do. Give him a little peck on the face, Reshma. I'll turn around.

RESHMA   I'm kissing him because I want to kiss him.

BEN   I don't care why you're doing it, just give the man a kiss.

RESHMA   Turn around.

KALYAN   This is absurd.

Ben turns around.

RESHMA   Goodnight Bunty. You're a great man. And you should get your own apartment.

KALYAN   Goodnight Reshma. I meant everything I said about your elbow and your tooth. I love them. I dream about your flaws.

BEN   Rein it in, brother!

RESHMA   Call me tomorrow?

KALYAN   First thing. Have a good night.

RESHMA   You too.

BEN   Can I turn back around now?

RESHMA   No.

BEN   I don't get a kiss?

Reshma exits.

BEN   That was kind of rude.

KALYAN   It was rude of *you*, Ben. You humiliated me.

BEN   Good cop, bad cop. I'm a dick and you look awesome by comparison. Which you are anyway, so I was just illuminating the truth of our dynamic. Anyway, you got some action, no need to thank me. Are you mad at me?

KALYAN   Well you did say you would be out—

BEN   Don't worry about it, no hard feelings. How was your date?

KALYAN   It was good and then a little weird.

BEN   Because I came home? You're gonna put this on me?

KALYAN   No, right before you came home, it got a little weird.

BEN   Probably because you were trying to teach her football on PowerPoint.

KALYAN   No, that part was fine. It was just she said that she didn't deserve me.

BEN   So?

KALYAN   She said it in a way that made me feel like there was something else going on.

BEN   Do you think it's because you're a faggot?

KALYAN   No. I don't, I mean . . . I mean I'm not. I mean that's not a word that should be used.

BEN   "I mean I mean I mean." Guess what I bought us? On the way home from the fucking life-sucking bar, I passed Curry Hill and picked up some Nepalese food.

KALYAN   Did you really?

BEN   Yeah, I figured you'd be hungry. Having not eaten any of Reshma. And that we could do a little cooking together.

KALYAN   Ben, that's so nice. And also crass and weird.

BEN   Now, I know you barbarians still like to eat with your hands, but we're eating with forks and knives and using napkins.

KALYAN   My grandfather would not be proud to see me using a fork. But this is a beautiful gesture.

BEN   It's a feast fit for the deposed King Gyanendra!

KALYAN   Ah, it sounds like someone's been reading a little about Nepalese history.

BEN   Guilty as charged, my friend. I love saying that man's name. Deposed King GYANENDRA!

KALYAN   Yes, he has a good name. Did you film anything today?

BEN   Nothing needed to be filmed.

KALYAN   'Cause I saw something I thought you might have liked. I know how you're always trying to capture real and dramatic moments for your film.

BEN   Not "dramatic." *Compelling.* There's a difference.

KALYAN   Well I saw this compelling situation I thought you might like. There was a man eating food out of a garbage bag he had clearly torn open himself. And then a dog ran up and started eating out of the same bag. And the guy didn't mind. They were eating the same food, the man and the dog. It was so strange and kind of disgusting, but also peaceful in a way that made me feel like we could all just coexist even in this gruesome way.

BEN   Wrap it, buddy. Long story short. Anything else?

KALYAN   Well, yes, I'm getting to it. This rich-looking woman approached and grabbed the dog away and yelled at it for eating the food from the garbage. She said something like, "Baxter, no! We don't eat from the garbage." She said "we" like Baxter the dog and she eat the same kind of food. But the food from the garbage was good enough for the homeless man. It was just so sad to see how human beings can value animals over another person, another human being, who happens to be a stranger. And I thought it might be interesting for your film.

BEN   All due respect, man, it's not really that interesting. I see stuff like that all the time and it's kind of cliché to show a sad homeless dude eating garbage.

KALYAN   I know it's probably not the most original thing in the world.

BEN   It's actually probably the most *un*original thing in the world. That's the problem with these fucking NYU assholes, they take a picture of a homeless man and call it art. It's like "Fuck you! That's not art! It might be art if *you* were homeless, but then you wouldn't be at fucking NYU, now would you?"

KALYAN That's true, you're right.

BEN I'm sorry to put down NYU. I know you're still happy there.

KALYAN Well, they didn't kick me out.

BEN Yeah, well you're in the business school, it's a much different pile of shit. And, hey, they didn't kick me out either! We had a mutual falling-out.

KALYAN I know you did.

BEN And the graduate department can suck my shit because they didn't know what they had on their hands with me. They didn't know how to think of me, what fucking little box to put me in. Well guess what?

KALYAN I don't know, what?

BEN When my movie comes out, I'll get a fucking honorary *PhD*. And don't think I won't accept it! I'll fucking accept it, yes, and I'll make a classy speech and say thank you and shake hands with those fuckwads, because if there's one thing I've learned from struggling it's that the best revenge is a life well lived.

KALYAN That's very sage.

BEN Thanks. Do you want some weed?

KALYAN No.

BEN No problem. I'm gonna smoke some nonetheless.

Ben relaxes on the couch, smoking, as Kalyan begins cleaning the house from his date.

BEN I had a kind of shitty day, Bunty. I mean, shitty compared to my other days, not compared to, like, world events.

KALYAN What happened?

BEN I'm crossing Third Avenue and I run into this kid I went to elementary school with, Ted. He said he's getting married. What a fucking douche bag, right?

KALYAN I don't know, is he? All I know is that he's named Ted and that he's getting married.

BEN He says to me, "Can you believe I'm actually getting married? Can you believe I'm finally settling down?" So I said, "Yes I can, you're a boring Jewy douche bag from New Jersey who never had a girlfriend. Of course I can believe you're settling down, what the fuck else are you gonna do, mow someone's lawn?"

KALYAN I hope you didn't actually say that.

BEN No, I said "congratulations." But I was thinking that pretty loud and clear. Ted got a job working on Wall Street. He's some kind of hotshot fuck or something. I don't know.

KALYAN Really? Do you know which firm?

BEN Yeah, I asked him for his whole life story. We were crossing the street, Kalyan, I didn't get into all that shit. Lay off.

KALYAN Well did you at least ask him if there was a job opening?

BEN You don't want to work on Wall Street.

KALYAN No, Ben, that is exactly where I want to work. Why do you think I'm here?

BEN You're here to learn. And you don't need a job. I told you, I don't want rent from you. Your money's no good here.

KALYAN I don't want to rely on you. I *want* to pay you rent.

BEN Fine! I'll ask him if there's a fucking job! Get off my jock. He gave me his number.

KALYAN Thank you. If it's a problem, just tell me.

BEN He actually wanted to hang out. He said, "We should get together for drinks." What kind of bourgeois bullshit is that? "Get

15

together for drinks." You never hear someone in the Democratic Republic of the fucking Congo ask someone to "get together for drinks."

KALYAN   Especially 'cause there's a drought.

BEN   That's actually funny, man. Your sense of humor is burgeoning.

KALYAN   I learn from the best.

BEN   I'm the best. Anyway, you wanna know the fucking kicker? The real salt in the wound of it all? You know who this guy's marrying? Sarah Newburg.

KALYAN   I don't know who that is.

BEN   The first girl I ever got an erection for! Sarah fucking Newburg.

KALYAN   Really? Your first crush?

BEN   It pisses me off, if I'm being honest. (*suddenly vulnerable*) It pisses me off, Bunty.

KALYAN (*gently*)   I know it does, man.

BEN   The world is unfair. You know that—you're from Nepal. But it's unfair here, too. I just feel . . . I just feel . . . like everything is fucked sometimes . . . Sarah was really nice to me.

KALYAN   It's gonna be okay.

BEN (*tough again*)   I know that. Anyway, she's probably ugly as shit by now, she probably turned into her mother—you know, all hips, no ass—but she was cute. If I'm being honest.

KALYAN   Are you jealous of Ted? It's okay if you are.

BEN   Jealous? Fuck no. He's an idiot. He's a banker. I'm actually doing something with my life. I don't have time for some bitch always in my ear, taking me away from my work.

KALYAN   You're going to do great things, Ben.

BEN Now, I'm not saying all bankers are idiots. But he's a fucking Jewish banker from New Jersey, a fucking Shylock, perpetuating stereotypes that, frankly, I don't need right now. It's different than you being in finance.

KALYAN How is it different?

BEN Look, it's kind of hard to describe because you're not from here. But if you're born in the States and you're white and you're fucking Jewish and you're middle class, banking is kind of seen as an easy way out. It doesn't have the nobility you think.

KALYAN I don't think it's necessarily *noble*. I wouldn't say *noble*. It's not any more or less noble than any other job, Ben. It's just an interesting field to me and a good way to make a living.

BEN Yeah, but here, for a Jewish kid from the suburbs, and I'm speaking as a Jewish kid from the suburbs, it's *not* interesting and it's a *shitty* way to make a living. Listen, it's like if I was born in Nepal like you, and I wanted to be a Sherpa or a Gurkha or a Parka or whatever, *that* would be like an easy way out, right?

KALYAN Gurkhas are considered the preeminent fighting squad in the world.

BEN And I'm sure they're great but—

KALYAN And Sherpas can summit Everest without oxygen.

BEN Again, a great accomplishment—

KALYAN Parkas keep you insulated from a cold breeze.

BEN That's cute. I'm just trying to say—and I'm trying to basically *not* insult you—The fact that you've come from Nepal, a fucking poor country—excuse me, a poor country—to the States to pursue a career in business is admirable in a way that for a fucking Jew—or excuse me, for a Jew—from New Jersey. Is predictable.

KALYAN What about movies?

BEN What the fuck about movies?

KALYAN   Well you want to make movies—I mean you *do* make movies. Isn't the movie industry disproportionately Jewish?

BEN   Yes, and I have two answers that I've already thought of because I think about this shit all the time. One is that I'm not going to be some rich fucking casting couch film executive and the other is that arts and cinema can reflect life and push boundaries in ways that moving money around to make more of it will never be able to! And I was getting a degree in film *theory*. I'll make a fucking *pittance* and I'm perfectly okay with that.

KALYAN   And you could always just borrow money from your father.

BEN   You want a hit?

KALYAN   Is it still marijuana?

BEN   Yes.

KALYAN   Then no.

BEN   My father's a prick. Can I tell you a secret?

KALYAN   Please.

BEN   Wait. Have I offended you with the banking comments? Because if I did, I'm sorry and I'm frankly also uncomfortable moving forward if I've offended you.

KALYAN   I'm not offended, man.

BEN   Because I couldn't live with myself, I'd actually fucking kill myself, if I've offended you in some way. I can't, like, move forward if I've hit a fucking animal in the road, you know what I mean? I can't keep driving thinking there's a dead animal behind us in the road, you know?

KALYAN   There's no dead animal. Keep going.

BEN   Because I think you're a fucking awesome person. And the fact that you're studying business at NYU and you're from Nepal makes you an awesome roommate and an awesome friend and I'm proud as shit that we know each other.

KALYAN I also feel proud of this relationship.

BEN You're a stand-up guy, Bunty. Okay, here's my secret. When I was eight years old, I had a dream about Sarah Newburg, this fuckface's new fiancée.

KALYAN Like a sex dream?

BEN More than a sex dream. Is it cool if I tell you something disgusting?

KALYAN I think so.

BEN Are you easily nauseated?

KALYAN In Kathmandu, I had giardia for four months. I have a strong stomach.

BEN I'm sorry to hear about your giardia.

KALYAN Thank you, it's all cleared up.

BEN Okay, when I was eight years old, I had this dream where I was lying on the floor of my second grade classroom. The desks were all pushed against the wall. And I had spread newspaper neatly all over the floor and was lying face up on the newspaper and naked. And here's the disgusting part. I'm kind of embarrassed to say it. Is it okay?

KALYAN It's fine, please go ahead.

BEN Sarah Newburg, the presumably respectable fiancée of the douche bag I just ran into, was standing over my face, straddling it, also naked, and shitting on me.

KALYAN She was defecating on you?

BEN On my face. I feel fucking awful about this. I've never told anyone before. I'm so mortified. Do you know what it's like to go through life with this image stuck in my dumb head, a naked eight-year-old girl shitting on my face? Am I awful?

KALYAN   Hmm. Let me think for one moment.

BEN   Take your time, buddy.

KALYAN   Okay. I think if you had that dream now and Sarah was still the eight-year-old girl, I think, yes, that would be awful. But seeing as you were both eight at the time of the dream, I think it's perfectly natural to have those kinds of fantasies. It's nothing to be ashamed of and frankly it's pretty brave to admit it.

BEN   Dude, how do you always know what to say to make me feel better?

KALYAN   I also have another thought that might make you feel better.

BEN   Another thought that might make me feel better! (*kisses his head*) I fucking love you!

KALYAN   I think it's very responsible the way you laid out the newspaper in your dream. It says a lot more about your character that you laid out newspaper to protect the floor of the classroom and to catch the fecal matter that, I take it, missed your face, than it does about your sexual deviancies. In fact, I don't think you need to be embarrassed about that dream at all. I think it shows great character and an ability to love another person despite their potentially off-putting bodily functions. The fact that she's doing that on your face and you still love her is very sweet and I think it means that you're going to make some other woman very happy one day.

BEN   Who the fuck are you? You are the most perfect person that exists! I've been haunted by this for 20 years!

KALYAN   Listen to me though, Ben. Having said all that, I do have one piece of advice you can either choose to heed or not to heed.

BEN   Yes, please! Advise! I'll heed, you perfect fucking specimen of a friend.

KALYAN If you're asked to make a speech at their upcoming wedding, I would leave this story out.

BEN You are the fucking best roommate I've ever had. You know that? You really fucking are!

Ben loudly plants a big kiss on Kalyan's head.

BEN And you know what? I'd love that Wall Street douche bag to meet you, I'd actually love that. My crazy Nepalese roommate! Let's get that fuck over here for some drinks!

Blackout. Wu-Tang Clan's "Method Man" angrily blares.

SCENE 2

Wu-Tang abruptly cuts out. Lights up:

TED *is looking around the apartment. Ben rolls a joint at the couch. Kalyan, dressed nicely, prepares crudités and beer.*

TED This is a sick place, you guys!

KALYAN Oh, this is Ben's place. I just rent the room.

BEN Well you *live* in the room. You haven't actually *rented* it in months. Let's watch the semantics, Bunty.

TED You must be doing really well, Ben. And this is all from film?

KALYAN Yeah, Ben's really talented.

BEN Hey, thanks buddy!

TED If you were able to swing this place, you must be talented.

BEN Times are good, brother.

TED Oh come on, you must've had some help from somewhere. All of our parents bought us apartments. I'm not ashamed. I've mostly paid my old man off anyway. Hey Kalyan, welcome to New York City, where all the kids are rich and no one can figure out how!

BEN   I thought your dad got cancer.

TED   He's been in remission for five years.

BEN   Weird.

TED   Yeah, in six months, he'll be out of the danger zone. Knock on wood.

BEN   So he didn't die?

TED   We spoke about an hour ago, so unless he got hit by a car or something—

BEN   It could happen. The world's a scary place. We're all just sitting around waiting to be killed.

TED   That's true, Ben. You always were a realist.

BEN   Always!

TED   Dude, I gotta say—I can't believe I'm here talking to you, it's so surreal. It is so nice to see you, man. You haven't aged a minute.

BEN   And you're in a suit!

KALYAN   Okay! We have some Crudités! And Nepalese Beer. The crudités was my idea. The Nepalese Beer was Ben's. I hope you don't mind Ted.

TED   No, I'd be down to try it. What kind of beer is it?

BEN   What kind? It's fucking beer, who cares what kind it is!

KALYAN   It's called Mustang, it's a lager. A pale lager.

BEN   I had an uncle who was a pale logger. Chopped his dick off one day cause he was drunk on Nepalese beer.

Ted laughs heartily as Kalyan passes out the beers.

KALYAN   Here you go Ted. And Ben.

TED   Okay! To old friends!

KALYAN   And new!

TED   Cheers!

BEN   Eh eh eh! It's Nepalese beer. We gotta say "Cheers" in Nepali! Show some respect. How do you say it, Kalyan?

KALYAN   In Nepali? I can't think of anything. I don't think we really have that.

TED   Come on, you must have something.

KALYAN   No, I don't think I ever said anything that would be an equivalent to "Cheers." I guess when we're drinking, we don't really feel a need to congratulate each other.

TED   You know, that's true, I never really thought about that. Why do people congratulate each other for drinking? It's not like it's a great accomplishment.

BEN   It's pure hedonism! Maybe, instead of saying "Cheers" like we've earned it, we should apologize to the world. Because they're all toiling away while we get to sit here and drink.

TED   I think that sounds like a better plan.

BEN   All right, raise your glasses, gentlemen. A Nepalese Cheers: To all the pathetic fucks breaking their backs while we drink this beautiful beer: I'm sorry!

TED and **KALYAN**   I'm sorry!

They clink their glasses, laughing.

TED   Ben, you're one of the funniest guys I've ever known.

BEN   "One of?"

TED   You gotta make a comedy movie. You don't like comedies? You could probably direct a really funny comedy movie.

BEN   Got any ideas?

TED I don't know, like what we just did! Like we were gonna say "Cheers" but then we decided that was selfish so instead we apologized. That would be like a funny little scene. It's not like a whole movie idea, but it's like a little scene, you know?

KALYAN That actually is a funny idea, Ben.

BEN Well, I'm already working on a different kind of movie.

TED Oh, sorry. Is it funny? What's the storyline?

KALYAN Tread lightly, Ted.

BEN I film whatever life presents to me and put it together in a new kind of art form that doesn't yet have a name.

TED Wow. Interesting. And, forgive me for being dense. But like, so, what do you actually film?

BEN Well, like just yesterday? I saw this dude eating from the garbage and a dog came up, started eating the shit too. And then this rich cunt comes up and takes the dog away, yelling at it: "Baxter, you can't eat from there!"—and the homeless dude keeps on eating.

TED Jesus, wow, you filmed that?

BEN Yeah, it's all stuff like that. And I'll put it into a compelling collage of life, or what you call a "Storyline."

TED That sounds cool.

KALYAN But remember how you also said that you liked how they were eating together at the beginning, the man and the dog? You said you thought it was peaceful, right?

BEN Nah, I didn't really like that part.

TED That sounds incredible, man. And I see what you mean, how that's more like, deep, than the comedy idea.

BEN Exactly. It's more deep. Like on a deeper level. Like, journey to the center of the earth and, boom, there's a homeless dude and dog sharing a plate of spaghetti.

TED (*trying to keep up*)   Like Lady and the Tramp?

BEN   Exactly!

TED   Ah, right!

KALYAN   So Ben said you're getting married?

TED   Yes, in June. We're really excited. In fact, Ben and Sarah and I were all friends when we were tiny.

BEN   You say that but I don't really remember her too well.

KALYAN   Was your announcement in the *newspaper*? Ben loves the newspaper.

TED   No, we're just doing a small private kind of thing. Immediate family, a few friends. One step up from City Hall.

BEN   He's only saying that so I don't feel bad that I'm not invited. Which I don't anyway.

KALYAN (*gently admonishing*)   Ben. (*to Ted*) So were you and Sarah high school sweethearts?

TED   Well we were, she just didn't know it. I was in love with her way before she even knew that I existed.

BEN   Ha!

KALYAN   No that's very sweet.

TED   In fact, when I first told her I loved her, you know what she said?

BEN   We weren't there, no.

KALYAN   What did she say?

TED   She said, "Thanks."

BEN   Face!

TED (*laughing*)   I know, it was awful. So you know what I did? I just started saying, "I love you, too" instead of "I love you."

KALYAN That's funny. The implication being that she's already said, "I love you."

TED Exactly. And it made her laugh. So now, every time I'm gonna say "I love you," I just say "I love you too." Or if she's the first one to say it, she'll say, "I love you too, Teddy." It's kind of become our thing.

KALYAN I really like that story.

BEN Me too. Can you tell it again but slower and could you lend me your sock so I can ejaculate into it?

KALYAN Stop it, Ben.

TED It's kind of sappy, I know. What about you guys? Are you dating, single? If it's not my business, just tell me to shut up.

BEN Okay, shut up.

TED Whoa. Sorry.

KALYAN Ben's kidding. That's his way of kidding.

BEN That's me!

TED No, I know how annoying it could be. The newly engaged guy asks you how your love life is, like suddenly, 'cause I'm getting married, the rest of the world is too.

BEN Exactly! It's annoying.

Ted laughs as Ben begins rolling his joint.

KALYAN Well, in answer to your question, I'm kind of seeing this amazing woman.

TED That's great, man.

KALYAN It is great. I'm just not really sure what it is, though. We like each other very much, but I could also tell that she's not yet ready to settle down.

TED Ah, like you know it's perfect, but she can't see it yet.

KALYAN   Right! And I have this recurring fear that I'm going to catch her on the street kissing someone else . . . some macho alpha male.

TED   I know the feeling.

KALYAN   She keeps saying that I'm too good for her. Like it's a bad thing. Like she secretly wants to date some guy who'll beat someone up at a bar for her.

TED   That's so funny. I totally get that. That's not us.

KALYAN   Exactly. I'm a pacifist. Literally. On my voter registration card, under "Party Affiliation," I wrote in "Pacifist." And I got in trouble for it. Ironically.

TED   Listen to me Kalyan, and I'm speaking from experience here. Guys like you and me? We win out in the end. She thinks she wants some bad boy and maybe she actually does now. But, in the end, girls want someone who'll take care of them. You're gonna be fine, man.

KALYAN   Thanks. I feel like I kind of know that, but I think I also need to be told sometimes.

BEN   I'm touched, you guys. And hard.

TED   So what about you, Ben? I feel like I don't know anything about you. You know, everyone kind of lost touch with you after high school. I know you went out west to school—film school, I guess?

BEN   No, for undergrad, I studied the humanities.

TED   Oh yeah? Which ones?

BEN   All of them. All the humanities.

KALYAN   Benjamin's become very humane since earning his bachelor's.

TED   That's funny.

Ben grabs his lighter and joint.

BEN   Can I spark up? Does anyone mind? Teddy, you back in the game?

TED   Sure, I'll take a little puff. It's been a long time. I used to get so paranoid, remember that, Ben?

BEN   Nah, not really. But this shit's good. You'll be fine.

TED   Thanks. (*takes a hit*) Wow. It's been a while.

BEN   Welcome back.

TED (*offers to Kalyan*)   Dude, you want some?

BEN   No, he doesn't smoke or do anything that's fun.

KALYAN   That's not true. This morning, I washed my socks and ate an omelet.

Ted chuckles.

BEN   That's not fun.

KALYAN   I know, I was kidding.

BEN (*slaps his head*)   Oh! Good joke! Anyway, elephant in the fucking room! Kalyan, tell him about yourself. Kalyan's doing amazing work.

TED   Oh yeah? What kind of work are you doing?

KALYAN   I'm currently getting a masters at NYU's Stern School of Business.

TED   Oh, you're an econ wonk like me! Stern's great. I went to Fuqua at Duke. It's a similar program.

KALYAN   Ah, yes, Duke. Go bulldogs!

TED   What?

KALYAN   Was your team not the bulldogs?

TED   No, we were the Blue Devils.

KALYAN   What am I thinking of?

TED   I'm not sure.

KALYAN   Blue Devils. Right. Duke.

BEN   Anwyay, Kalyan's the real deal. You know, he wrote a book. Can you believe it? He wrote a fucking book. Big hit in Nepal, he's like the Harry Potter of Nepal.

KALYAN   It was not such a big hit.

BEN   And so modest. Unlike Harry!

KALYAN   Ben said you work at a big firm. May I ask which one?

TED   Yeah, sure. I'm at White Rock. Do you know it?

KALYAN   Of course I know it. How long have you been there?

TED   Almost ten years. I started interning right out of high school and worked remotely through undergrad and they half paid for my MBA at Duke. It's kind of like a family for me; I feel like I never actually *worked* a day in my life.

BEN   That's funny. Me neither.

KALYAN   I know a lot about your company. For a big investment house, you guys are doing some amazing work with mirco-loans.

TED   Yeah. The boys do all sorts of stuff like that. It's partly PR—

KALYAN   No, that's cool, that's neat. It's kind of my area of expertise.

TED   Really? What are you studying?

KALYAN   Well, it's an MBA. But the program's called "Social Problem-Based Entrepreneurship," so I'm trying to reconcile collectivization in the developing world with the effect it has on international markets.

BEN Kalyan, you're boring the life out of us white folk! Can I show him your book? I'm like a proud parent or something. This is embarrassing!

Ben goes to his messy bookshelf and begins rooting through it to find the book.

BEN He got a scholarship from his school in Kathmandu to study in the States so that he can go back to Nepal and save it from itself.

TED That's great man.

KALYAN Well, actually I'd like to get a little experience working, frankly, where you work. White Rock is such an important company right now.

BEN Fuck that, he doesn't want to work on Wall Street. You don't want to work on Wall Street. He's gonna go back to Nepal, degree in hand, and save that place.

TED You know, I can get you an interview with someone, if you wouldn't mind starting in Asset Management. It sounds like you're past it or just interested in different things—

KALYAN No, that's fine, that's great! I just want some real world experience.

BEN Real world experience? You're from fucking Nee-Pal! What's more real world than DEPOSED KING GYANENDRA!?

KALYAN Ben, can you please stop screaming that man's name? He terrified my country for seven years.

BEN Sure, sorry. Anyway, you gotta go back to Nepal. Otherwise you're just adding to the fucking brain drain. They sent you here to learn and, on graduation day, you're flying your educated gray ass back to that shit-hole of a country—excuse me, that country—and saving it!

KALYAN Thank you for planning out my whole life, Ben.

BEN No problem, buddy.

KALYAN   I was trying sarcasm.

BEN   Well done!

TED   Are you sure you guys are roommates?

BEN   Nope!

KALYAN   Yes, we are. What do you mean?

TED   Well you kind of act like a married couple.

BEN   We only act like that when we're not fucking.

TED   (*laughing*)   No, seriously, how do you guys know each other?

KALYAN   I posted an ad looking for a room on an NYU message board.

BEN   It was terse and devoid of character, just like Bunty. "Room needed. I am clean, responsible and keep normal hours."

KALYAN   So we were perfect for each other.

BEN   Yeah!

KALYAN   I was trying sarcasm again.

BEN   It's going well. Lilt your voice a little more and then we'll be able to tell. Hey Ted, you wanna hear something fucked?

TED   Sure.

BEN   When I met this kid, he was delivering pizzas. He wrote a hit book in Nepal, comes to New York to study and the fucking dumb capitalist system has him delivering pizzas to stoned idiots.

KALYAN   I never minded delivery. Nothing wrong with an honest job.

TED   Nothing at all.

BEN   Well, the man's a genius. And I recognized it and took him in immediately.

Ben finds Kalyan's book, throws it to Ted.

31

BEN   Here it is! You're gonna love this shit, Teddy.

KALYAN   Ben, have you actually read it since the last time you hadn't read it?

BEN   I'll get to it, you know how proud I am of you.

KALYAN   I do know that, I'm kidding.

Ben sits on the couch and smokes. Ted takes a look at the book, reads the back cover.

TED   This is interesting. So you're making a connection between a drought, a political uprising, and a decline in international tea sales. You know, I think there are some guys at work who'd be interested in checking this out. Do you mind if I borrow it?

KALYAN   Mind? I'd be honored. Unless, I don't know, Ben, were you planning on reading this tonight?

BEN   I might. Toss it over here, Tedster?

Ted walks over and hands Ben the book. Ben thumbs through it.

BEN   Yeah, I may read it tonight. I'll give it to you when I'm done, though.

KALYAN   Are you serious?

BEN   Yeah, man. I'm sorry I haven't supported you. I'm a shitty friend sometimes. Teddy, you want another hit?

TED   No thanks, man.

BEN   I can be a shit sometimes. I probably have some anger deep down but it comes out as shit. And I procrastinate like a motherfucker. Jesus Christ, do I procrastinate. So I'm sorry I haven't read the book.

TED   Do you guys maybe have another copy of the book?

KALYAN   No, unfortunately. My family has a few copies in Nepal. But it's out of print.

BEN You know what?

Ben recklessly throws Ted the book.

BEN Teddy, you take the book.

TED Okay, thanks man.

KALYAN Thank you Ben.

BEN Don't thank me. I can't wait to read it.

KALYAN Hey, can I give you my email or something?

TED That'd be great. Here: just type it on my phone. Send yourself an email, so this way you have mine too.

Ted gives Kalyan his phone. Kalyan begins typing.

BEN This is adorable. It's like a fucking first date. Bunty doesn't do shit on the first date.

TED Are you sure? I can be pretty charming.

BEN I know. You're marrying that girl, what's-her-name.

TED Sarah's-her-name.

BEN Right, Sarah. I think we went to school together.

TED You know your mothers still see each other all the time.

BEN That makes one of us.

TED I know that Sarah would love to see you Ben. She still talks about you.

BEN (*mocking*) Wow! Still?!

TED Yeah, she's always saying how creative you were and how interesting you are. Probably cause she's marrying a boring guy like me.

BEN Probably.

TED You know what? We should all have dinner together.

KALYAN   That would be great!

BEN   I don't know, man. I'm pretty busy for the next several years.

TED   We're all doing shit, but we're never too busy for friends. Come on! What about the five of us?

BEN   You're pretty bad at counting for someone on Wall Street. Who's five?

TED   Me and Sarah. Kalyan and his girl. And you.

BEN   Well that sounds like it would be a blast for me.

KALYAN   You know, I think Reshma would probably like that.

TED   Then let's do it. Ben, you let us know if you're down. And we'll plan it. This is gonna be great, I know Sarah's gonna be psyched.

BEN   That's the most important thing.

TED   Take care you guys. Great to see you Ben. Your movie sounds really cool.

BEN   Oh yeah, it's gonna be supercool. Neato!

TED   And Kalyan, we'll just stay in touch. Great to meet you.

KALYAN   You too. Thank you again for considering the book. And, like I said, I'd be happy to do anything at the company. Or just an interview, if possible. Or a casual meeting. Really. Anything.

BEN   Can you please suck his dick in the other room?

TED (*jokey*)   No, here's fine.

BEN   Eww. Jesus, Teddy. Get your mind out of the gutter.

TED (*laughing*)   You're hysterical man. Really. Always a pleasure. Always!

  Ted leaves.

BEN   What a dick, am I right?

KALYAN   I really liked him.

BEN   Me too, I'm just kidding around.

KALYAN   Yeah, he's really cool. It's nice to meet people like him who've really made it.

BEN   "Made it?" How has he made it? He's had one job his whole life.

KALYAN   It's impressive to stay at a competitive firm like that for so many years.

BEN   No, it's lazy. Hey. Are you offended by my actions this evening?

KALYAN   Which ones?

BEN   You knew what I was doing with the book, right?

KALYAN   You mean how you pretended you were going to read it tonight?

BEN   Yeah, you know why I did that, right?

KALYAN   Well, I thought you actually wanted to read it.

BEN   No, no. I was just playing hard to get. Like if he thought he couldn't have your last copy, he'd want it even more. That's why I gave it back to him.

KALYAN   Oh, I thought you might actually finally read it.

BEN   You wouldn't want that.

KALYAN   Yes, I would, Ben.

BEN   Why? What the hell can I do for you?

KALYAN   You're my friend. And my roommate. I want you to be interested in what I'm doing.

BEN   You need to have more confidence in yourself, man. You shouldn't worry so much about what other people think of you.

KALYAN   You used to read all my papers. You loved them and made little comments in the margins and proofread everything.

BEN I've gotten busy.

KALYAN No you haven't.

BEN Hey! We're all a little tense right now! Cool it down!

KALYAN What is your problem Ben?

BEN I saw her cunt.

KALYAN Excuse me?

BEN I saw his fiancée's cunt.

KALYAN Are you talking about Sarah?

BEN I'm talking about her cunt. Can I tell you a secret about Sarah and me?

KALYAN How many of these do you have?

BEN I have a few. Can I tell you about that? About when I saw her cunt?

KALYAN Ben, I don't know.

BEN Please. Can I tell you?

KALYAN Okay, fine. But can we not call it that?

BEN What?

KALYAN Her . . . genital. Can you please not call it the "C" word?

BEN What should we call it?

KALYAN I'm not planning on calling it anything. It's your story. So what happened? And was this a dream or did it really happen?

BEN No, this really happened. I used to be friends with a kind of aggressive kid named Warren. And we were like seven years old. It was around the time that Sarah shat on my face, but definitely beforehand, which makes sense because I don't think I would have been able to dream about her naked had I not actually seen it.

KALYAN   You're a class act.

BEN   Thank you. So we were playing in Warren's bedroom, some dumb game, like *Guess Who?*, which you probably don't know because it's American so just picture checkers or Nepalese pickup sticks or whatever. And her parents come to pick her up and they honk the horn outside, in the driveway. And she gets up to go and Warren says that she can only leave if she shows us her cunt—sorry, her genital. So she pulls down her pants a little bit and fucking shows it to us!

KALYAN   Oh my god, Ben. I don't know if I could hear about this.

BEN   Hey, where's the tact you showed me during the shitting story?

KALYAN   Okay, I'll try to look past the sexual exploitation of a child.

BEN   We were all kids, settle down. So her pants and panties are stretched down to reveal her thing and we are just looking at this fucking new image, this thing we'd never seen before or, if we had seen it before, we were looking at it in a whole new way. And I was horrified a bit, because it was so audacious of Warren.

KALYAN   Warren sounds like a troubled kid.

BEN   Warren didn't make it past the age of twelve.

KALYAN   What happened?

BEN   He died.

KALYAN   What?

BEN   But that's not important right now. What's important is that, while she's showing us her genital and her parents are honking the horn outside, Warren just looks down at the ground, like he's embarrassed or something. Weird, right?

KALYAN   Weird, but also understandable. It's a shocking experience.

BEN But I, who didn't ask to see it, who never would have thought to ask to see that, stare at it. I can't take my eyes away.

KALYAN Interesting.

BEN Don't judge me.

KALYAN I'm not.

BEN I remember that it was the most exhilarating feeling I'd ever had. My heart was racing. I was sweating. I was so turned on by it. Even at seven, I felt sexual feelings that were real and intense. But it was more than sexual. I think I was actually in love.

KALYAN Are you serious?

BEN Yes, and I think that was the last time I was really in love. I know that must sound perverse. Why am I telling you this?

KALYAN It's okay, man.

BEN Is it?

KALYAN Yes.

BEN That was the last thing I ever saw that really made me feel like I wanted to love something. And I think I still might be in love. Isn't that fucked?

KALYAN I think it might be a little unhealthy, yes.

BEN Do you think I would make it in Nepal?

KALYAN Make it?

BEN Yeah, I always thought you and I were so similar. But I don't know that I'd be able to cut it there, you know? And you had to actually *live* there, like every day.

KALYAN Ben, I think you'd be fine anywhere you went.

BEN Do you really think that?

KALYAN I really do.

BEN   Thanks Kalyan.

KALYAN   No problem.

BEN   Hey Kalyan?

KALYAN   Yeah buddy?

BEN   Do you think she would like me?

KALYAN   Who?

BEN   You know.

KALYAN   Sarah?

BEN   Yeah.

KALYAN   I think she would like you. Ted said that she always thought you were so interesting.

BEN   He did?

KALYAN   Yeah, he said Sarah thinks you're so smart and talented and creative.

BEN   Yeah, he did say that. I wonder if she'd still think that.

KALYAN   You've got a lot going for you.

BEN   Do you think it would be a good idea to ask her to come over for dinner? We could cook the Nepalese food I bought the other day. I think Sarah might think it's interesting, seeing everything I have going on in my life.

KALYAN   I think she'd probably want to bring Ted over.

BEN   You think she really likes him?

KALYAN   I imagine she does, yeah.

BEN   Fuck. You're my only friend.

KALYAN   I know.

BEN   It's so strange. You're not gonna leave me ever, right?

KALYAN   I don't see how I possibly could.

BEN   Me neither. Could you hug me for a second?

Kalyan hugs Ben.

BEN (*sadly*)   I think I got really stoned.

KALYAN   It's okay, man.

Kalyan stays hugging Ben. Lights fade.

SCENE 3

A cheesy instrumental version of Billy Joel's "Scenes from an Italian Restaurant" plays from a tinny computer. A PowerPoint presentation is illuminated. The slides read:

Welcome Reshma, Ben, Sarah and Ted to your first Nepalese Dinner.

What follows is a general introduction to my cuisine and some guidelines to eating Nepalese food.

Most importantly: Don't Freak Out!

Yes, we will be having a "traditional" Nepalese dinner.

But you'll notice that the word "traditional" was in quotes.

The quotes should make you feel safe.

The quotes mean it's not really going to be traditional.

In fact, as a precaution, always look for quotation marks around words like "traditional," "authentic," and "home style" when eating Nepalese food.

This lets you know that you will not get giardia or amoebic dysentery.

We will be eating a variety of foods tonight.

They may remind you of Indian foods . . .

But we don't like this comparison.

RESHMA   Hey!

No offense Reshma.

RESHMA   Thank you.

We will be eating Dal Bhat Tarkari.

This is a staple Nepali dish that will not make you puke.

We will also be eating Chatamari.

This is like Nepalese Pizza and will also
not make you puke.

Finally, we will be eating Masu.

This is a curried spiced meat dish and,
if you do puke, this is why.

And most importantly . . .

You need to know that Nepalese people, regardless of class,
eat with their hands.

That's right. Your friend Kalyan . . .

A picture of a smiling Kalyan.

. . . who you allow to sleep in your homes . . .

A picture of Kalyan in bed.

. . . grew up eating with his hands.

A picture of Kalyan eating with his hands.

I Nepal-ogize for any stomach or body odor problems
that occur as a result of tonight's experience.

BEN And there's the pun!

Don't comment on my puns, Ben.

SARAH Oh! Burned by PowerPoint, Ben.

BEN Ouch.

The End!

Lights fully up on Reshma, Ben, Sarah, and Ted. They politely applaud. The table is beautifully set.

SARAH Dude, that was fucking hysterical.

BEN He's my roommate!

RESHMA You are such a geek.

KALYAN Better to be a geek than to disappoint your guests with unfamiliar cuisine.

TED Is that an ancient Nepalese proverb?

BEN No, he just made it up now.

TED "Better to be a geek," says Buddah!

BEN We got it, Teddy.

KALYAN Okay, first things first. Despite my compelling sales pitch, who here would still like to use utensils?

TED I'm definitely using a fork! Sarah?

SARAH Hell no! I'd love to use my hands.

BEN Sarah! Up top for Hands.

Ben slaps Sarah five.

TED Okay, the lady hath spoken. We will both be using our hands!

BEN That was a quick turnaround.

SARAH I can be very persuasive.

BEN Your man's got a strong backbone, there, Sarah.

SARAH Not anymore, Ben. I've whipped him too many times.

TED Oh! Is that why I wake up sore in the morning?

SARAH That's one reason.

RESHMA I am not using my hands!

KALYAN Okay. Ben?

BEN Are you fucking kidding me? I'd eat with my hands anyway! Just like you, Sarah. I'd eat with my hands even if they were fucking tied behind my back and there was a gun to my head and the only way I could avoid being shot was to pick up a fucking fork. I'd still eat with my hands!

SARAH Wow. That's a dramatic hypothetical situation, Ben!

BEN I'm a dramatic man, Sarah.

KALYAN Okay. So that's four hands and one fork!

TED (*to Reshma*) Hey, if we all eat with our hands, there'll be less dishes to clean.

SARAH That's my man! Always thinking of a practical reason to do something fun!

RESHMA Sounds just like Kalyan!

KALYAN Hey! I'm fun.

RESHMA You're a lot of things, but fun?

TED We're not fun! Embrace it, Kalyan! We're left-brained freaks.

BEN You guys sound like a blast! (*mock-checks his watch*) "Well, it's the first of the month, honey, time to fuck!"

SARAH That's totally Ted!

TED That is me! I love you too.

SARAH I love you too.

BEN There it is.

Ben watches as Sarah pecks Ted on the lips. Reshma looks at Kalyan.

RESHMA Did you pick up the wine?

KALYAN I didn't have time after class. But it's fine. We have something better: Nepalese beer!

RESHMA I'll probably just have water.

KALYAN Resh, what's wrong?

RESHMA Nothing. It's fine. It's just, I asked you to pick up the wine.

TED Is it the beer we had on Thursday?

KALYAN Yes, Mustang. Is that all right?

TED Yeah, it's great. Sweetie, I think you'll like this.

SARAH What kind of beer is it?

TED It's like a pale lager.

SARAH Oh cool. I'd be down to try it.

BEN Sarah, I had an uncle who was a pale logger. He actually chopped his dick off one time when he was drunk on Nepalese beer.

SARAH You are insane!

RESHMA That is actually funny, Ben. I'm shocked.

BEN It's a true story.

SARAH I'm sure.

BEN You don't believe me?

SARAH I've never believed you, Ben.

RESHMA Should we move to the table?

KALYAN Yes! Definitely. Resh, should we pass out food or just let everyone help themselves?

RESHMA Everyone should just take, it's annoying when you get more than you want.

KALYAN Great. Everybody to the table, please!

BEN Like cattle, we march!

Sarah tries to help Reshma carry food to the table:

SARAH Do you need help carrying anything?

RESHMA No, no! Sit! Please!

Sarah moves to the table. Kalyan tries to help Reshma:

KALYAN Can I help you?

RESHMA It's a little late.

KALYAN Sorry.

RESHMA Just go sit down. I got it.

Reshma carries the dishes to the table. They all sit down.

SARAH This looks great, you guys.

TED Yeah! It looks hearty.

BEN That sounds like a euphemism.

TED Hey, Ben, Kalyan, should we show the girls our Nepalese Cheers?

SARAH What's a Nepalese Cheers?

TED Ben had the funniest idea. We asked Kalyan how you say Cheers in Nepalese—

KALYAN And I said that we didn't have an equivalent.

SARAH (*to Reshma*) How do you say it in India?

RESHMA   I have no clue. I've never been there.

TED   So we were thinking that it's so strange that people—

BEN   Wait, you've never been to India?

RESHMA   No.

BEN   Weird.

RESHMA   Why is that weird?

BEN   Uh . . . because you're fucking Indian?

RESHMA   Where do your grandparents come from?

BEN   Moldova.

RESHMA   Have you been to Moldova?

BEN   Fuck no, I've never been to Moldova, but if they were from somewhere cool like India I'd be on the first flight out. You gotta get more in touch with your roots.

RESHMA   Thanks for the advice, grasshopper.

TED   Anyway! We were thinking that the Nepalese people don't say "Cheers" because it's weird to congratulate yourself for just drinking alcohol. Right?

SARAH   That's actually a really good point.

TED   Right, so Ben said that we should say, "I'm Sorry" to all the people that are working while we're drinking.

RESHMA   Ben! Showing a little humanity for a change.

BEN   It's in me somewhere.

TED   And I thought it would be like a funny idea for one of his movies, you know? You can picture it: a group of people sitting around and instead of saying "Cheers," they say, "I'm sorry." It's funny.

SARAH   So let's do it!

Sarah raises her glass. The others follow.

SARAH   To the huddled masses from polluted sea to polluted sea: I'm sorry.

KALYAN, TED, RESHMA, BEN   I'm sorry.

BEN   Sarah, you're the coolest girl I know.

RESHMA   Hey, thanks, Ben.

BEN   No problem. So, Sarah, what have you been up to all these years?

TED   Didn't I tell you when we ran into each other on the street?

BEN   I had a lot going on that day, Teddy, I wasn't exactly taking notes on our interaction!

SARAH   Ted remembers everything, so he assumes everyone else does. I teach math at a school for court-involved youth.

KALYAN   Wow, what does that mean, "court-involved youth?"

SARAH   When kids are arrested, one of two things can happen. They can either go to what we think of as a prison—it has bars, they're in uniform, the whole nine. Or they can go to group homes, where they live with a communal guardian and get bused to my school every day. It's called an "alternative to detention" school.

KALYAN   Wow. That sounds intense. But amazing.

SARAH   Well, it's just a regular teaching job for me.

TED   No it's not. She's being humble.

BEN   Hey, let the woman speak.

TED   Sorry, honey.

SARAH   No, it is. For me it's just teaching math, but with the added benefit of knowing I'm enriching the minds of some kids who really need it.

RESHMA   So what are they in for?

TED   Let's just say that all of her students know the metric system.

KALYAN   What does that mean?

RESHMA   He means because they deal drugs. Like a gram of weed, a kilo of coke . . .

KALYAN   Oh. Really?

TED   Nah, it's just a stupid joke.

BEN   It's not *just* a stupid joke. It's also gauche and racist.

Ted laughs.

RESHMA   So what are they in for?

SARAH   I never ask.

RESHMA   But you must be curious.

SARAH   You know, I was at first. When I first started teaching, I would just stare at these kids from the front of the classroom and wonder—did Raymond, who's sitting in the back of the class in his Knicks hat, kill someone? Did little Michelle who knows her seven times tables scratch some other girl's face off? Or shoplift? Or curse out a cop on the subway? And once, I actually snuck into the principal's office during lunch and peeked into folders to see the profiles on these kids. And what I read shocked me. And I went back to class knowing that Raymond did in fact kill someone and Michelle scratched the face off her little sister after drinking a bottle of mouthwash. But I immediately felt something else, something so strong and so distinct that it shocked me even more than what I had just read.

Sarah takes a swig of beer, leaving everyone on the edge of their seats . . .

RESHMA   What?!

SARAH   I discovered that I just didn't care. It didn't matter what they did and I was just kind of disgusted at myself for knowing. I looked at Raymond and I looked at Michelle and, even knowing what I knew, they looked the same. They looked like kids in a math class. They were here now. We were in this room together. And we were learning math.

KALYAN   Wow.

RESHMA   What an amazing story.

BEN   I was never good at math.

SARAH   It's a little cheesy, I know.

RESHMA   It's not cheesy at all. I wish I had someone like you as a teacher.

TED   And Reshma, Kalyan told me how amazing you are.

RESHMA   Did he?

KALYAN   I may have said a little something.

TED   Oh yeah. He wouldn't stop talking about you.

SARAH   What do you do? I know that's kind of lame to ask.

RESHMA   No, it's not lame at all, it's my life. I'm in med school?

BEN   Is that a question?

RESHMA   No it's not. I'm in med school.

KALYAN   Reshma is a lifesaver.

BEN   There we are! Not to be outdone!

RESHMA   I'm not really a lifesaver. I mean I *was* a lifesaver. But now, I mostly study the diseased tissue of dead people. I'm doing my rotations at Weill Cornell and last week they had me in the ER saving lives. But now I'm in pathology.

TED   What's pathology?

RESHMA   It's studying how diseases affect the body, so mostly I'm working with diseased tissue from . . . well basically from dead people.

KALYAN   Reshma's probably the only person in the world that actually longs to be back in an Emergency Room.

RESHMA   That's true! It totally suited my personality. The pace, the excitement, the adrenaline. And I guess I also loved telling people that I save lives during the day. But I have to say, and I don't want to sound morbid, I also kind of love working with dead people.

KALYAN   You see? This is why we get along so well.

BEN   That was almost funny, dude.

KALYAN   Thanks, Ben.

BEN   No problem. Work on your timing.

RESHMA   And I guess I had a kind of revelation similar to yours, Sarah.

KALYAN   What revelation? You didn't tell me you had a revelation.

RESHMA   No, it was just this revelation that I love my job. For the right reasons. Like how you found that you liked teaching math for its own sake. I kind of found that the other day.

SARAH   What happened?

RESHMA   Well, this kid came in, he was killed in what I think was a gang-related thing. And he'd been shot in the chest three times and there were three distinct bullet holes in his body.

BEN   Normally I don't like to hear these kinds of stories when I'm eating, but this is actually making the Masu taste better.

RESHMA   So I was thinking, if this kid was shot last week, I probably would have seen him in the ER. And at first I felt guilty, like if only I could've saved him . . .

TED   Of course.

RESHMA   And I started thinking that pathology was such a stupid, meaningless rotation for me. But then I realized without cutting this guy's body open—Sorry! That's totally gruesome.

SARAH *(rapt)*   No, keep going.

KALYAN *(rapt)*   It's okay.

TED *(rapt)*   Yeah. Don't worry.

RESHMA   Without *examining* this guy and learning what happens to a body when a bullet gets lodged in your spleen after entering through your stomach, we wouldn't know how to save the next guy that comes in with the same thing. And I got a rush from it! And it's not the same rush you get from running around a bloody ER, but just the rush from feeling like you're part of something bigger than yourself and something that's actually, in a real way, maybe important.

BEN   Hakuna Matata!

TED   Kalyan, are we the luckiest men in the world, or what?

BEN   "Or what!"

TED *(laughing)*   Hey! Come on!

BEN   I'm just kidding. You're both lucky. I just think it's a little obnoxious.

TED   Obnoxious? What's obnoxious? What did I say?

BEN   It's just, Sarah tells this incredible story of how she's like helping these criminals learn math—I mean it really was a wonderful story, Sarah—and then Reshma has to jump right in with her own tale of heroism. It's just kind of obnoxious.

KALYAN   Ben.

RESHMA   Are you serious?

BEN   It was Sarah's moment is all.

SARAH   Ben, it wasn't my moment. I mean, we were all just talking.

BEN   Oh. Then I'm just kidding around. It was a beautiful story, Reshie.

TED Oh! Jesus Christ, man. You kind of scared me. I can't tell when you're kidding.

BEN I'm totally kidding. I mean, it makes sense that Reshma would tell that story. Indians are very competitive people.

RESHMA Excuse me. What the fuck?

BEN What? Your culture strives to be the best. It's not a criticism. It's a great thing.

RESHMA It's offensive.

BEN How is it offensive? What did you get on the SAT, Reshma? What score did you get?

RESHMA I'm not telling you.

BEN But you know what the score was, right?

RESHMA Yes, I know.

BEN Right. Ted, what did you get?

TED I don't know man. I don't remember.

BEN See? (*points at Reshma*) Indian? Competitive. (*points at Ted*) White dude? Doesn't even remember his SAT score.

KALYAN Hey, Ben. Why don't you cool down a minute?

BEN I'm cool right here. I'm gonna get some more beer.

Ben walks over to the fridge and picks out five beers.

RESHMA What the fuck is his problem?

KALYAN Just let it pass. I'll talk to him later.

RESHMA You mean after he's blacked out? That's very helpful.

BEN Who's up for round two? Teddy? You in?

TED No thanks for me. I'm still working on this one.

SARAH Yeah, me too.

BEN All right. More for me.

Ben opens his second beer and chugs it at the fridge, putting the empty back in.

SARAH So Ben, do you want to tell us about your movies?

BEN Yeah! I had this amazing revelation last week. I was making a movie and I realized that I just like working with dead people and kids and it was so beautiful and the world is so good!

SARAH Come on, be serious. I was really hoping to hear about them.

BEN You were, Sarah?

SARAH Yes! I guess Ted didn't tell you that I really love movies. Like probably the same kinds as you.

TED Sarah watches the strangest movies.

SARAH I do, I have weird taste. I don't really like the regular stuff in the theaters.

BEN Any movie that's commercially released is necessarily a piece of shit!

SARAH That's so funny! Sometimes I actually think that.

BEN I always think that!

SARAH Well, it's your industry. So you would know. I'm only an audience member. But I'm just attracted to the weirdest stuff.

TED Just to be clear, she's not talking about pornography films or anything. She just likes, what? Independent films? I guess like Ben's. Which we still haven't seen!

SARAH Yeah, Ben, I really want to see your movies. I'm embarrassed to say this 'cause it's totally stalker-y, but I actually looked you up online when I heard you were directing movies. Because I wanted to see what you've done. But there was nothing listed.

BEN   Yeah, I took all of that online stuff down. Because I didn't like the way online reviewers can just write anything anonymously.

KALYAN   You've gotten some amazing reviews though.

BEN   That's true. He's right, I have, Sarah. Thanks, Kalyan.

SARAH   So you were able to take everything offline? I didn't even know you could do that.

BEN   I prefer to work under the radar, it's just more pure.

TED   I didn't think it's possible to take stuff offline.

RESHMA   I think you have to have the same IP address that posted whatever was up in the first place.

BEN   Yeah, I got all that IP stuff.

KALYAN (*saving Ben*)   Reshma also likes smaller-type movies. What was that one you were just telling me about?

RESHMA   Oh my god—yeah. Did you guys see *Martin's Fall*?

SARAH   It sounds familiar. Is that about the guy with the leg? I read something about it.

RESHMA   Yeah. It's about this guy who has one leg but you don't realize it till the end.

BEN   Well thanks for keeping it a surprise!

TED   Yeah, now we don't have to see it! Right, Ben?

RESHMA   But that's the thing, it doesn't really matter if you know or not. About his leg. Because it's about so much more than that.

TED   I'm just kidding around. It sounds interesting.

BEN   Does it?

RESHMA   It's really just about this guy, this human being, suffering a loss. And the leg could be anything, really. And the guy could be anyone. It's like it's a story about everything and nothing at the same time.

SARAH   See, Ben? That's the kind of stuff I like.

TED   "*Martin's Fall*"? I'll definitely check that out. Is there a bathroom I could use?

KALYAN   Yes, of course.

RESHMA   I'll show you.

Reshma begins to lead Ted out.

SARAH   So Ben, how do you decide what stories to tell?

Ted suddenly reappears.

TED   Oh, I'll field that! Ben just filmed this homeless guy eating out of the same garbage bag as a dog. And then this rich woman starts yelling at the dog for eating out of the garbage. Isn't that incredible? He's a like a real renegade.

Ted ducks into the bathroom, Reshma checks a message away from the table.

SARAH   You filmed that?

BEN   Yeah, I filmed that.

SARAH   Wow. I didn't realize you do documentaries as well!

BEN   I could do anything that you like, Sarah.

SARAH   That footage sounds incredible. It's like that's the whole point of movies, right? A hundred years ago, before there was anything being filmed, you could only *read* about something like that, which was interesting, but not as objective as seeing it. The expression on the homeless man's face, the ravenous dog, the mean woman who you could also see yourself in. Ben, that's why what you're doing is so important and it is renegade, in a way. I would love to see that, if you're comfortable showing us.

KALYAN   Oh, I don't think that's fully edited yet, right Ben?

BEN   No, it's fully edited. I just can't show it. Because I've submitted it to a few festivals. And I only had the one copy.

SARAH   I would absolutely love to see that sometime. I really would. When you get it back, please call me.

BEN   Okay, maybe I will. Maybe I will, Sarah.

Ben chokes up, suddenly emotional.

BEN   Would you excuse me for a minute?

Ben stands up and wobbles unsteadily to his bedroom, as Ted and Reshma reemerge.

RESHMA   What's he doing?

KALYAN   I don't know.

SARAH   Is he always like this?

RESHMA   Yes.

KALYAN   Well, he's getting worse. But he means well.

RESHMA   He's a dick. He's harmless, but he's a dick.

TED   I think it's good that we're here.

SARAH   Yeah, me too.

They sit in silence. Kalyan sniffs the air.

KALYAN   Do you smell that?

SARAH   Oh yeah.

KALYAN   He's smoking.

TED   I didn't tell you. We smoked weed the other day. When I came by here.

SARAH   Why didn't you tell me that?

Kalyan (Kunal Nayyar) shows Reshma (Annapurna Sriram) his PowerPoint presentation on American football.

Ben (Jesse Eisenberg) tells Kalyan about his dream.

Ted (Michael Zegen) on his first visit to Ben and Kalyan's apartment.

Sarah (Erin Darke), Ted, Reshma, Kalyan, and Ben
eat Nepalese food together.

Ben tells Sarah about his dream.

Ben destroys Kalyan's book.

Kalyan pays Ben back.

Sarah tells Ben about his good deed.

TED   I mean I didn't inhale, are you kidding? That stuff used to make me so paranoid. But I didn't want to be rude, so I just took like a little puff and passed it back.

KALYAN   I used to do that too, until he caught on and stopped offering.

BEN (*OS*)   Are you guys talking about me?!

KALYAN   No! Are you okay Ben?

BEN (*OS*)   I'll be out in a minute! Don't talk about me, okay?

KALYAN   We won't.

BEN (*mumbles, OS*)   Be out in a minute.

There is an uncomfortable silence as they decide what to discuss instead.

TED   So, Kalyan actually wrote a book.

SARAH   Really? Like fiction, nonfiction?

KALYAN   Nonfiction. Very nonfiction. Economics.

RESHMA   It's about the economy of Nepal. And it's really interesting and insightful.

KALYAN   Yeah, I gave it to Ted.

TED   I read it a few days ago. Really interesting. The stuff about the villagers?

KALYAN   The Tribesmen?

TED   The Tribesmen! Yeah, really interesting stuff.

KALYAN   Wow, thank you so much!

RESHMA   You see what happens when you put yourself out there? He thinks he's burdening people by asking for help.

TED   No, it's no problem.

SARAH Never a burden!

TED To be honest, it's not really my area. But I gave it to some guys at the office. Do you need it back pretty soon?

KALYAN Well, whenever they're done I guess. Or they can keep it if they want to.

Ben returns with his pipe. He is stoned and stumbly.

BEN Does anyone want some weed? I found some in the drawer where I keep my weed.

They just stare at him, not sure how to take it.

BEN Don't judge me.

KALYAN No one's judging you, buddy.

Kalyan stands and helps Ben walk back to the table.

KALYAN Let's just sit back down.

BEN I am, I am. I don't need help sitting at my own table, man. Okay? You're the one who—who needs—It's *my* table—

KALYAN It is. Okay.

RESHMA So! Who wants dessert?

KALYAN Yes! Dessert!

They move to the coffee table, where Reshma sets a plate of cookies and sliced oranges.

RESHMA Coffee? Tea?

SARAH Sure, tea would be great.

TED Make it two.

SARAH Well, one each.

TED Right!

RESHMA One each!

TED Are these ancient Nepalese chocolate chip cookies?

KALYAN Yes, carved from the foothills of the Entenmann Mountains.

Ted cracks up. Ben provocatively moves his chair toward the group. They all turn.

BEN Sarah! It is so good to fuck-ing see you. Do you know that? Sarah and I used to be friends. Well not really friends. But we were tight.

SARAH Yeah, we were all really good friends. You, me and Teddy.

BEN Teddy was a weird kid though.

TED We were all a little strange.

BEN But you were exceptional.

TED Thanks Ben.

BEN You don't know everything about me and Teddy, do you Sarah?

SARAH Do you guys have a dark side I don't know about?

BEN We all have a dark side. Some people are just too embarrassed to show it.

TED Ben, what the hell are you talking about?

BEN You know what I'm talking about, man.

RESHMA Kalyan, you want to do something?

KALYAN Ben, why don't you go lie down for a bit?

BEN Where? In *your* bed?!

KALYAN Ben!

BEN Hey! We all had a turn to tell our story. Now it's my turn.

SARAH Okay, yeah, he's right. Tell us your story, Ben.

Ben takes a hit off his pipe.

BEN   When we were twelve years old, Teddy and I killed someone.

TED   Excuse me?

BEN   We killed an innocent kid named Warren, who wanted nothing out of life.

TED   Who's Warren?

BEN   Well no one now, brother!

TED   That sounds more like a movie idea than real life, Ben. Maybe you should put that in a movie.

BEN   You know what I don't need from you Tedster? Another fucking movie idea! I don't come to your office with ideas about how to move money around, do I?

SARAH   You don't remember Warren Shepherd? He was that kid who put Elmer's glue in his hair to make a Mohawk in like second grade.

TED   Oh! Warren *Shepherd*! That's right, he did die.

BEN   Now he remembers!

TED   I barely even knew that kid.

BEN   I guess you don't remember sixth grade then. March 13th, which just happened to be a Friday the thirteenth, Teddy and I are in Bio. It's about 9:15 in the morning, second period. Warren shows up late to class. The teacher, Mr. Price, asks Warren where he's been and Warren says, "Your mother's house." And Teddy laughs. A little too loudly I guess because Warren swings around and points at Ted. None of this sounds familiar to you? Warren points right at Ted and says "Don't fucking laugh at me." And storms out of the room.

TED   I have absolutely zero recollection of that.

BEN I thought you're supposed to be the one with the great memory.

TED Well maybe it never happened.

BEN No it happened. And it gets worse. After Warren leaves, Mr. Price goes back to teaching and Teddy leans over to me and says—and I'll never forget this—our kind, little, sweet little Teddy says, "Warren's such an asshole. You know, if Warren died, I wouldn't be upset."

TED I said that?

BEN And then that summer, in the woods behind school, Warren fucking died.

SARAH I thought he overdosed on something, right?

BEN He was huffing paint thinner. Alone, in the woods behind school.

SARAH That's right, how horrible.

TED And you're blaming me?

BEN I'm blaming both of us! Because when you said that you wouldn't be upset if Warren died—

TED —Which I don't remember saying—

BEN When Teddy said "I wouldn't be upset if Warren died," I just sat there like a fucking stooge, saying nothing.

SARAH But what could you have said?

BEN Oh, I don't know—Like "Maybe you *would* be upset if Warren died." Or "Maybe you shouldn't have laughed at a kid who's obviously in horrible pain. Who runs away from his home every week! Who smells like shit because he doesn't shower! Who no one likes! Who's crying out in fucking pain for someone—for *anyone* to acknowledge him! To make some fucking normal eye contact with him to show him that we know he's alive!"

The group is quieted.

BEN   But instead, I sat there silent, like a complacent idiot. With blood on my hands. And I know it's probably easy for you guys to dismiss things that make you uncomfortable. But it's not so easy for me.

SARAH   Ben, that's not fair.

BEN   No, I remember that you guys started getting a little popular in junior high and Warren was just a little inconvenient blemish, right? Just a little collateral damage wiped out so the fucking cream can rise to the top.

RESHMA   OK, that's enough of that. Guys, do you wanna go somewhere else? Maybe we can head out to a bar or somewhere we won't be assaulted.

SARAH   Ben, what made you think of this boy?

BEN   The boy is not the point! *The point is* . . . The point is . . . You cannot just go through life happy and popular. Okay? People cannot just *go through life* . . . *happy!* And shut the rest of the world out.

Pause.

TED   We weren't even that popular!

SARAH   That's not the point he's making, Ted.

TED   So what *is* the point? I still don't understand how any of this makes sense.

SARAH   Just let it go, Ted.

TED   No, you can't just draw weird conclusions like that.

BEN   So how come we never talked about it again, man?

TED   Uh—because it was a fucking irrelevant moment?

SARAH   Ted, you're doing the wrong thing right now.

TED No, you're just *choosing* to remember it in this weird way. You didn't do anything wrong! And I certainly didn't do anything wrong.

BEN So why did you say it then? Why did you say, "I wouldn't be upset if he died"?

TED If I did, it was probably because I was *twelve*! Who even remembers something like that?

BEN *I* do! *That's the point! I* remember something like that!

The group is silenced. Ben runs to the kitchen, speaks in hushed tones.

BEN Kalyan, could you come here for a sec?

KALYAN Sure buddy.

BEN Did I cause a ruckus?

KALYAN I don't know what that word means.

BEN I think it's from a song.

KALYAN Yeah, I don't know that song.

SARAH Ben, maybe you should have some water.

BEN I think I had a bad childhood when I was younger.

SARAH No, I was there, you didn't.

KALYAN Let's just go to your room. We'll take a little rest. I'll come with you.

BEN You'll stay with me?

KALYAN I'll come with you. Take my hand.

BEN I'm sorry everybody.

KALYAN Let's go.

BEN Good night Sarah.

SARAH Goodnight Ben.

BEN Do you like the house?

SARAH Yeah, it's really nice.

BEN It's mine.

Ben and Kalyan exit to the bedroom.

RESHMA Okay, it's fucking 8:30. I'm not going home. Where should we go?

SARAH I don't know. Maybe we should just head home. Teddy?

TED You guys work it out. I'm done arguing for tonight.

RESHMA I spent my week in a hospital, I'm not spending my night in a morgue.

SARAH Maybe we should stay here. Do you think he's okay?

RESHMA Girl, how are you not eaten alive by those students you teach?

TED She's too sweet. I'm always telling her.

SARAH All right. Maybe I could get a glass of something.

RESHMA Or a bottle. You guys go downstairs. Wait for me. Get a taxi.

Reshma opens the door and pushes them out as Kalyan reenters.

RESHMA Bunty, come on, we're heading out.

KALYAN I think I should stay.

RESHMA I think you definitely should not.

KALYAN I should wash the dishes.

Reshma exits. Kalyan looks around. He picks up a few plates from the table and brings them to the sink. He heads back toward the table but stops and looks at the front door. He looks back toward Ben's bedroom.

Kalyan walks to the front door, grabs his keys, shuts out the light and exits. Blackout.

ACT 2

One Week Later

The projector illuminates the following raw film footage as the lights slowly fade up.

A nicely dressed 60-year-old woman yells at a small dog. She says, "Baxter, no! We don't eat from the garbage."

We hear Ben, off camera, say, "Try it again. More angry."

The woman says, "No Baxter!" Ben says, "Angrier!"

The woman says, with great anger and terrible acting, "Baxter, NO! We don't eat from the garbage!"

Ben says, off camera, "Great! Cut!"

The lights fully fade up to reveal Ben sitting on the couch editing this scene on his laptop and drinking a red bull.

He rewinds the footage and watches it again. He edits out the first two takes and plays the last one. He then cues up another shot:

Angle on a dog eating from the garbage. It's an amateurish looking close-up of the dog gnawing at the trash bag. We hear Ben off camera yelling at the dog.

"Tear into it! Really go for it! Can somebody please put his nose in deeper?" The dog's nose gets pushed in the garbage by someone off camera. Ben says "Great, perfect! Cut!"

Ben, on the couch, takes a swig of Red Bull and takes a deep breath, satisfied.

Ben hears keys starting to open the door so he closes his laptop and runs offstage, into his bedroom.

The door opens and Kalyan, Reshma, Ted, and Sarah enter. They are giddy and drunk.

SARAH   So, I saw this dog the other day. It was a collie. But just like a regular collie, which was weird . . .

TED   Hmm. I can't believe it's not border!

They all crack up at the inside joke.

SARAH   How'd you know that's where I was going?

TED (*a funny demon voice*)   I know all!

RESHMA   I thought you were gonna say I can't believe it's not breeder!

SARAH   What does that even mean?

RESHMA   I have no idea. I was gonna say I can't believe it's not better!

They laugh again.

TED   Wait, do we have to be quiet?

RESHMA   Is Ben home?

KALYAN   I'll check.

RESHMA   If he is, I'm leaving.

SARAH   I would say hi.

KALYAN   He's actually been amazing the last few days.

SARAH   What do you mean?

KALYAN   He started working on some project after you guys were here last week and he's been a totally different person.

Ben exits from his bedroom. He is in good spirits.

BEN   Namaste, motherfuckers!

TED   Did we wake you up?

BEN   Are you kidding? I've been slogging away all night.

RESHMA   You're actually working?

BEN   Yes I am, Reshma, I don't take weekends off, like some people.

KALYAN   Is it okay if we're all here now or are we in your way?

BEN   No, I was hoping you guys would come back here! Seriously, I'm good. I could use a little break.

SARAH   Are you sure? It's getting so late.

RESHMA   I know it's almost morning and I can't believe it's not brighter.

The gang cracks up!

BEN   What's so funny?

RESHMA   Nothing, it's stupid.

TED   Ben, we brought you some food back from PJ's.

BEN   Awesome. Thanks! What'd you bring me?

TED   It's a veggie burger.

SARAH   Kalyan said you like it from that place.

BEN   Perfect. I love it. Thanks guys.

Ted goes to the fridge and pulls out the Nepalese beer.

TED   Ben, you want a beer?

BEN   No thanks. I try not to drink when I'm working.

KALYAN   Have you just been editing all night?

BEN   Yes, sir. I've actually gotten a lot done. It's so great to be working again! To be creative in life!

TED   That's amazing. "The director at work!"

SARAH   It's so cool that you can edit at home. I like this beer. Although I don't remember it being so sweet. I can't believe it's not bitter.

They all crack up again! Ted runs to the sink to do a spit take.

BEN   What are you guys laughing at?

TED   Can we please just tell him?

RESHMA   It'll probably be so stupid if we try to explain it to you.

BEN   Try me.

SARAH   It is so stupid!

TED   No it's not. It's funny.

SARAH   Okay, so Kalyan never heard of that stuff "I Can't Believe It's Not Butter."

KALYAN   I can't believe I've never heard of that.

They laugh again.

SARAH   So we started thinking of like other things—how did it even start?

RESHMA   I can't remember exactly, but we all started saying things that ended with "I Can't Believe It's Not Butter," but changing it a little bit. Like this guy goes to the doctor because he's pissing blood and the doctor says, "You have a kidney infection." So the guy says, "But I'm pissing blood. Are you sure it's a kidney infection? I can't believe it's not bladder."

BEN   Ah, I see.

KALYAN   That was one of the more creative ones.

TED   Clutch play, Reshie!

SARAH   And then Ted did one that no one got until he explained it.

BEN   The best kind of jokes are the ones that need an explanation.

SARAH   I love you too Teddy, but you need to update your humor, honey.

TED   I love you too. What was my joke?

RESHMA   Don't pretend like you don't remember.

TED   Okay. It was something like, "Did you hear what happened to the guy who pretended to be Cal Ripkin Junior? He snuck onto the field and grabbed a bat. And he struck out, didn't hit one ball. And then the umpire took a look at the guy, saw that it wasn't Cal Ripkin and said, 'I can't believe it's not batter.'" I know, it's terrible.

SARAH   See Ben? It's totally stupid.

Ben stands up, playful.

BEN   No, it's not stupid. In fact, it reminds me of a story. An "I Can't Believe It's Not Butter" story.

SARAH   Oh really?

TED   Bring it!

KALYAN   Ben, as my humor instructor, you better not make me look bad.

BEN   Okay. So this guy is in a sexless marriage. And he's tried everything. Couples' counseling, pills, sex toys, nothing works.

RESHMA   Okay. Ew.

BEN   Hey, let me finish. So one day, he walks into his backyard and sees a time machine.

KALYAN   I like this already.

BEN   So he decides to go back in time to when prostitution was legal, because he doesn't want to break the law but he's desperate for some human contact.

TED   Of course.

SARAH What do you mean, "Of course"?

BEN So he sets the time machine to like Civil War times because he figures prostitution was probably rampant during the war. But right before he presses the big red button to go back in time, he runs back into his house and grabs his wife's diamond earrings.

SARAH Why does he get the earrings?

BEN You'll see. Wait for it. So the guy goes back to 1862 and he gets out of the time machine and he's dodging gunfire and muskets and all this racist shit and he finds a bar and he asks the bartender "Where can a guy get a woman around here?" And the bartender's kind of a grizzly old guy with a shotgun and he says, "Brothel's right upstairs." So the guy asks for the most beautiful woman they have and says, "Money is no object." So the bartender sends him into Mary Todd's room—

RESHMA Wait, sorry. The prostitute's name is Mary Todd?

BEN Yes it is.

RESHMA That was Abraham Lincoln's wife's name.

BEN Well it was a popular name at the time. But this one's a different chick. And she's a virgin.

SARAH Oh of course! Mary Todd, the virgin hooker of 1862!

BEN Exactly!

RESHMA Is this going somewhere?

BEN Did they ask Beethoven if his Ninth was going somewhere? You're looking at a master storyteller, Reshma.

RESHMA Okay. Keep going.

TED Yeah, I wanna see what happens to MT!

BEN So the guy goes upstairs and makes love to Mary Todd. And it's beautiful. They climax vocally and simultaneously.

SARAH You're a real romantic, Ben.

BEN Thank you, Sarah. So the guy gets dressed and walks back down to the bar to pay. And the grizzly old bartender says "One virginity of Mary Todd? That'll be 45 dollars." Now the guy only has modern money, which is meaningless in 1862, so he pulls out— Sarah! What does he pull out?

SARAH Oh! The earrings!

BEN His wife's diamond earrings! And places them on the bar. But the bartender says, "That don't look like no 45 bucks to me." And the guy says, "Won't you accept them in exchange for the sex?" But the bartender says, "Cash only. No exchanges." So the guy says, "Well I guess I can't pay then." And the bartender loses his shit. He grabs the shotgun, points it at the guy and says, "Mary Todd's my daughter. And you took her virginity and you don't even have money to pay for it. Now you're gonna die. Do you have any last words?" And the guy thinks for a second and then he says, "Yes I do. Back home, I'm in a sexless, stale marriage. And I really thought I'd be able to come back to 1862 and exchange these earrings for one night with a beautiful woman like Mary Todd. But I didn't realize you were only accepting paper currency. So call me old-fashioned but, before you kill me, I really must confess something about this economic system: I can't believe it's not barter!"

The group bursts out laughing.

KALYAN My roommate, ladies and gentlemen! My roommate! And life coach! And humor teacher!

RESHMA Ben, you're a sexist pig, but I apologize for all the times I called you stupid.

BEN You never called me stupid.

RESHMA I do in my head every time I see you.

BEN Ouch!

RESHMA I have to pee. Keep celebrating!

Reshma exits to the bathroom.

SARAH   Ben, you are a fucking genius!

TED   I can't believe it's not fucking *barter*! Seriously, why don't you do stand-up comedy?

BEN   I don't know.

TED   But you're funny! I mean, how many people are *actually* funny?

BEN   Maybe a dozen.

TED   See? Even *that's* funny! You could totally do stand-up.

SARAH   Teddy, just because someone is funny doesn't mean they have to immediately go out and make a living from it.

TED   Yeah, but he's in the arts. So I'm just trying to think of other things he could do.

BEN   I feel pretty satisfied with what I'm working on now, actually.

TED   I know. I'm just saying . . .

KALYAN   So what have you been working on? Can we get a little sneak preview?

BEN   Oh, I wish. I just don't think it's ready.

SARAH   You'll have to invite us to the premiere then.

BEN   Actually, Sarah, I've been editing that scene you told me you wanted to see. Coincidentally. Remember you said you were interested in seeing the scene I shot of the homeless man eating from the same garbage as the dog?

SARAH   Yeah! I'd love to see that, but I thought you said it was away at some film festival or something?

BEN   Oh, yeah. It was, but I got it back and I'm re-editing it.

KALYAN   Ben, are you sure that's what you've been editing?

BEN   Yeah, it's coming along great!

72

KALYAN How, exactly, have you been editing that particular scene?

BEN Uh . . . with the footage I shot?

KALYAN (*confused*) Interesting.

BEN Yeah, it is really interesting. I was just re-cutting some of it because I wanted to de-emphasize the harshness of the rich woman. In the cut I sent, she comes off a little too angry.

SARAH Right, because I guess, even in documentaries, you're shaping the reality.

BEN What do you mean?

SARAH The way it's framed, edited, the context, you're always shaping it according to your own perspective.

BEN Exactly. You know, I think I should be finished by tomorrow if you want to come by after school to watch it.

SARAH Oh! Yeah, I think we can come by. Teddy?

TED I can't—Kalyan's coming by the office after work for his interview. I'll actually be home a little late.

KALYAN Ted got them to squeeze me in after hours.

TED I pulled a little string or two.

BEN So then, I guess it's just us.

SARAH Right. Okay, sure.

BEN And maybe you could give me some notes. And even work on it with me, in a way.

SARAH You would want me to do that?

BEN Yeah, I could really use some fresh eyes!

TED I didn't tell you about his interview?

SARAH No. Who's he meeting with?

KALYAN It's with Michael Baron?

BEN (*to Kalyan*) That's great, man. (*to Sarah*) So I'll see you tomorrow then!

SARAH Yes! Definitely! Tomorrow. (*to Kalyan*) Mike's a great guy. He'll love you.

KALYAN I hope so.

SARAH I mean, he's a doofus.

KALYAN Doofuses love me.

SARAH I just mean, you're brilliant and interesting and he's a jock floating by on nepotism.

TED If Kalyan took advantage of nepotism, he'd be planting turnips in a field in Nepal right now.

KALYAN Hey! My father didn't plant turnips!

TED Oh no? What was it?

KALYAN Actually, it was turnips.

Reshma re-enters from the bathroom.

RESHMA You didn't tell me your interview was tomorrow.

TED (*singsong*) She's ba-ack!

KALYAN I didn't tell you?

RESHMA Are you prepared?

TED He doesn't need to prepare anything.

SARAH Mike'll probably be playing online poker during the interview. Kalyan's fine.

RESHMA No, I mean we've been out drinking all night, I just don't know if that's the best foot forward.

TED Okay, Kalyan, when you're at the interview tomorrow, don't mention that you were out drinking.

RESHMA   Maybe I'm being too tough, I just want to make sure you present well. It's an important interview. Did he read your book?

KALYAN   I guess I'll find out tomorrow.

RESHMA   What? I just want him to do his best. He never asks for anything and he's one of the few people that actually deserves to.

TED   He'll be fine.

RESHMA   Am I being a bitch?

KALYAN   No, not at all.

RESHMA   I'm asking Sarah. Am I being a bitch?

SARAH   Um . . . like the tiniest bit.

RESHMA   Thank you! See? I just need to be told.

SARAH   Kalyan would be the sharpest guy in that tool shed. Trust me, he'll be fine.

RESHMA   Sorry sweetie. (*kisses Kalyan*) But if you don't get that job, you can delete my number from your phone.

BEN   Ow!

KALYAN   Wait, really?

SARAH   Okay, now you're being a bitch.

RESHMA   I'm kidding! Mostly.

TED   Come on, Ben! Have one beer.

SARAH   To celebrate your new film and Kalyan's new job.

KALYAN   New job *interview*. It's just an interview!

SARAH   Okay! To celebrate your new film and Kalyan's new job *interview*!

BEN   Okay! Fuck it! Gimme a beer!

Ted grabs a beer from the fridge and tosses it to Ben.

SARAH Ben! As the clear winner of I Can't Believe It's Not Butter, you gotta give us a Nepalese Cheers.

BEN Okay, okay! To all of those who aren't drinking this delicious Nepalese beer. To all of those who don't have people in their lives who love them and who they love. To all of those who don't have creative and professional pursuits that enrich their lives and get them out of bed every morning. To all of those who aren't us: I'm sorry.

They clink bottles.

Blackout.

SCENE 2

In the transition, Ben giddily sets up a screening for Sarah. He throws a bag of popcorn into the microwave. As it heats up, popping, he prepares the house for her:

He sets up a chair with a makeshift ottoman. He cleans the apartment and sets a small bouquet of flowers on the table.

Finally, he sets the bowl of microwave popcorn and a glass of ginger ale on the table. Sarah enters and sits down. Ben starts playing the film:

The homeless man eats from the garbage as Baxter the dog runs up and starts eating from the same bag. The rich woman approaches.

She screams, "Baxter, No! We don't eat from the garbage!" The camera cuts to the close-up of the dog gnawing at the bag. The woman grabs the dog away. The camera cuts to a shot of the homeless man, who is clearly an actor playing a homeless man, sadly watching the dog leave.

Ben watches Sarah nervously. Sarah is inscrutable and she does not touch her popcorn.

The camera cuts again to see a long angle of the woman huffing and walking away. Then back to the homeless man, who frowns and bites a donut from the garbage can. It's clear that this is a staged scene amateurishly concocted.

The film fades out on a shitty zoom in to the homeless man's sad face.

The screen goes blank. Ben runs over and switches on the lights. Sarah is perplexed.

BEN   It's just a rough cut. I'm still tinkering with some of the dog stuff. I think it's a little much, but people want to see everything these days. You can't be too subtle, which is such a shame, in a way.

SARAH   Right ...

BEN   Did you think she was too mean? I'm struggling to figure out who our protagonist is. You can't have a mean protagonist but if they're too perfect then they have nowhere to go. You know?

SARAH (*carefully*)   I don't think she's too mean.

BEN   Great! I needed a woman's perspective. I get too wrapped up in the minutiae of every moment, it's easy to lose the macro.

SARAH   She seemed fine.

BEN   But she's provocative enough for you to want to see more, right?

SARAH   Right.

BEN   Yeah, that's what I think too. It's like, "She's a bitch, but maybe she can change." I think the most interesting characters are initially difficult to like, which is why I think she's more Charles Foster Kane than George Bailey and that's something I'm fine with. Do you like your soda?

SARAH   What?

BEN   I didn't know if you like soda, so I bought ginger ale, which seemed like good a compromise.

SARAH   Right. Thanks. It's fine. Can I ask you a question?

BEN   You can ask me anything you want.

SARAH   Did you actually film this?

BEN Yeah, but a while ago. It's weird revisiting it.

SARAH No, I mean did this really happen?

BEN Yeah, on 17th Street.

SARAH I thought you said it was a documentary.

BEN Yeah.

SARAH So how did you get all those shots?

BEN What do you mean?

SARAH I mean, like, how did you get the close-ups of the dog and the homeless man if it was a documentary?

BEN I took some artistic liberties.

SARAH So you told me it was real, when actually you manufactured it.

BEN Are you calling me a liar?

SARAH I don't know. Are you lying to me?

BEN It's like a hybrid.

SARAH Why would you lie about that?

BEN What's the difference if something really happened or not? It still exists somewhere, in my mind/on the street, it's real in some way.

SARAH No, it's not Ben. You implied that you randomly came across this scene and filmed it and now you're telling me that you didn't. Why would you do that?

BEN Because I wanted to impress you.

SARAH Oh.

BEN Yeah.

SARAH I didn't realize.

BEN Are you impressed?

SARAH   I think I'd be more impressed if you actually filmed them.

BEN   Why?

SARAH   I don't know. I guess because that's what you said you did and lying to me is off-putting.

BEN   I'm off-putting to you?

SARAH   Don't twist my words.

BEN   Do you think you'd want to work with me on it in some way?

SARAH   In what way?

BEN   I don't know. Like we could get together and make it more real. Or something.

SARAH   Ben, I feel betrayed a bit. I'm feeling a little dumb right now.

BEN   Don't feel dumb. I did this for you! When you said that you wanted to see it, I went out and filmed it for you.

SARAH   So when you told Teddy you filmed that scene on the street, you actually hadn't filmed anything at all?

BEN   No. Isn't that sweet?

SARAH   No. But do you see why that's not sweet? It's unfair. It's like you took a shortcut that you shouldn't be allowed to take.

BEN   Why shouldn't I be allowed to take it?

SARAH   Because it's dishonest. Because if everyone took shortcuts like that the world would be chaotic.

BEN   The world is chaotic!

SARAH   Maybe yours is. But mine isn't. In fact, I've tried very hard to make sure my world is in order.

BEN   Okay, let me just explain what happened.

SARAH   Okay. Explain.

BEN   I . . . This is difficult. I've been having a little trouble getting everything started. Like, with my life.

SARAH   I know.

BEN   You do?

SARAH   Well you said that you deleted everything on the Internet about yourself.

BEN   That was actually true.

SARAH   Was it?

BEN   No it was also a lie. But the truth is, Sarah, I've been having trouble with so many things. And when I saw you last week, at dinner, everything started feeling, I don't know, *possible* again.

SARAH   I'm glad you feel that way, but that probably has less to do with me than you think.

BEN   No, it has everything to do with you.

SARAH   That's just not possible. Don't you see how that's not possible?

BEN   Do you remember me?

SARAH   What do you mean?

BEN   Like from school? I used to think about you so much. Do you remember me?

SARAH   Of course I remember you.

BEN   What do you remember? Was I interesting? Was I funny?

SARAH   You were funny, yeah.

BEN   I did something funny?

SARAH   Yeah, I'll never forget this thing, and I was just reminding Ted, I think in third grade, Mr. Thomas said something like, "You know, Ben, if I made a list of every person who didn't do their homework, you'd be at the top of the list."

BEN   And I said something funny back?

SARAH   Without missing a beat! You said, "Do I get a prize?"

BEN   I did?

SARAH   Yeah, it was audacious. But really funny. I still remember that.

BEN   But did I ever do anything *interesting*?

SARAH   Interesting? Like what?

BEN   Like did I ever do anything memorable? Besides just talking back to a teacher.

SARAH   I'm not really sure what you're looking for. Did *I* ever do anything interesting?

BEN   Every day.

SARAH   Really? Like what?

BEN   Like when you brought new pencils in for everyone when we had that midyear test in Mrs. Reynolds's class.

SARAH   That's right! How do you remember that?

BEN   'Cause you said you brought them in for good luck, which was so nice.

SARAH   But didn't half the class fail that test?

BEN   Yeah, but maybe if you didn't bring them in, the whole class would have failed.

SARAH   Maybe.

BEN   And when all the cheerleaders decided to wear short skirts every time there was a home game and you started wearing those thick orange woolen pants that came up to, like, way over your stomach.

SARAH Oh my god! How do you even know about that?

BEN Because I used to think the cheerleaders were hot, but when I saw you silently rebelling against those sluts by wearing your grandmother's clothes, I thought you were awesome.

SARAH I don't even think I knew what I was doing.

BEN I did. But did you like me? What do kids think of each other?

SARAH Yeah, I thought you were great, I don't know. I guess kids don't really think about other kids in that way.

BEN I thought about you. In that way.

Pause.

SARAH Ben, come on.

BEN Sarah. I think I love you. I think I can't love someone else.

SARAH Ben, I'm getting married.

BEN I know. I'm just telling you a feeling.

SARAH I kind of thought you might feel that way.

BEN Is it obvious?

SARAH A little.

BEN Does Ted know about us?

SARAH No, Teddy's not a suspicious person. He doesn't think about things like that.

BEN I'm sorry.

SARAH It's okay to have those feelings. And it's very sweet to tell me about them. But it's probably best if you can feel them for someone else. Someone who would be able to love you back in the right way.

BEN   I don't think I can, though.

SARAH   Yes you can.

BEN   It's hard to describe. It's been a long time . . . You're the only person I know in the world, Sarah.

SARAH   Ben, we haven't seen each other in ten years.

BEN   But I've loved you since I was five years old! I've loved you even before I knew what that was!

SARAH   I don't know how you see me, but it doesn't feel very real. Do you know what I mean?

BEN   When I was younger, I had a dream about you. Can I tell you what happened?

SARAH   Do I want to know about this?

BEN   I need to tell you. You were doing something . . . very intimate with me.

SARAH   Like a sex dream?

BEN   It was more than a sex dream. It was something very strange.

SARAH   Do you feel like you need to tell me?

BEN   Please, yes! It was in Ms. Parness's classroom. I pushed the desks against the walls and I spread newspaper neatly over the floor and you were naked, I'm sorry, but you were naked—

SARAH   That's okay.

BEN   And I was also naked so it's not that weird.

SARAH   It's okay if you weren't.

BEN   But I was! We were both vulnerable. And me even more so because you were standing over me, straddling my face and . . . can I say it?

SARAH   Say what?

BEN You were shitting on me.

SARAH Oh.

BEN And it wasn't perfect, clean balls of feces, it was messy, a little soft and sometimes soupy and it was going in my eyes and in my mouth and it was slimy on my neck so I could feel it when I moved my head. And I was looking up at you I was seeing the feces coming out of your body and it was so gentle and real and nice. And I was just showering in you.

SARAH Ben I don't think—

BEN No! It was beautiful. I wiped it from my face and rubbed it on my body. All over my body. I wanted to bathe in it. And you kept on going. Like shitting was just an activity you could choose to do for as long as you want. You gave me as much shit as I could handle. And I wiped it on my thighs and on my chest and on my penis. And I had an erection but I didn't know what to do with it. I just knew that blood was flowing to every part of my body and I felt more alive in that dream than I've felt in the last twenty years.

SARAH Why are you telling me this?

BEN Because it made me love you even more.

SARAH Ben, this is a lot to hear.

BEN Are you disgusted with me?

SARAH No. I don't know. It's sad.

BEN It is?

SARAH Yeah, but it's also nice.

BEN It *is* nice! Does Ted dream about that?

SARAH I don't think he would tell me if he did.

BEN So marry *ME*, Sarah! How do you not like me? I'm so interesting! I'm interested in films, like you. And I know about art and being depressed and I'm comfortable with people from all over and I listen to rap and I'm hard to pin down! Marry Me!

SARAH Ben, I like you, but I'm not marrying Teddy because he's interesting.

BEN Obviously.

SARAH I'm marrying him because I love him.

BEN But what the fuck does that even mean? Why can't you love me? It's all just arbitrary! You love him/you love me/you love the Beatles/you hate the Beatles. It's all just fucking arbitrary!

SARAH It's not just about sharing interests. If I wanted someone with my interests I would have married Jenny Greenfield, you remember her?

BEN We had bio together. She had a lisp.

SARAH But we had all the same interests. I'm marrying Ted because he loves me back in an adult way. In a real way. He takes care of me.

BEN Don't you think that I could take care of you?

SARAH I don't know. Maybe you could. But I'm already engaged.

BEN But you can become unengaged! I become unengaged any time someone starts talking about sports. It's easy.

SARAH That's very cute.

BEN You're very cute.

SARAH Thank you.

BEN You're beautiful, I think.

SARAH Thank you Ben.

He buries his head in her lap. She freezes.

SARAH I'm going to leave now, okay?

BEN Okay.

SARAH I want you to sit up first.

He stays down.

SARAH You have to sit up.

He doesn't move.

SARAH Benjamin. Sit up.

He sits up, looking away.

BEN No one calls me that anymore.

SARAH It's okay.

BEN Should I lean in to kiss you? I don't know what's happening.

SARAH Benjamin.

BEN Is that what's happening to us? Is this that time?

SARAH No, it's not.

BEN Are you sure? Maybe I lean into kiss you and you remember that this was the time I leaned in and everything changed. Please tell me!

SARAH That's not what's happening.

BEN Is it because I ruined the moment by asking you if I should do it?

SARAH No, that's not why.

BEN I'm sorry I lied about the movie.

Ben leans in to kiss her. She pulls away.

SARAH Please don't do this.

BEN I love you too.

He leans in again.

SARAH   Please stop.

BEN   Say it. I love you too.

SARAH   Okay, I have to go.

BEN   I love you too!

SARAH   You're being manipulative.

BEN   You're being a bitch.

SARAH   Do not call me a bitch!

BEN   Sorry, I didn't know.

Sarah brings her glass to the sink. Ben tries to take it from her.

BEN   No! Please don't leave! I didn't mean to lie about the movie!

SARAH   You can't just tell someone this kind of shit and expect them to not have any reaction. You can't just expect me to sit here and not be . . .

BEN   Be what?

SARAH   I don't know! It's just too much to hear!

BEN   But it was all nice things!

SARAH   Saying nice things isn't always the nice thing to do!

BEN   Why not?

SARAH   Because it's selfish! It is selfish to tell someone that kind of stuff when they're not in a place to reciprocate. And the fact that you can't see that is even more upsetting—

BEN   I wasn't trying to be selfish!

SARAH   Good luck with your movie.

He grabs at the glass. She pulls it back and he tears it away from her and throws it against the wall, shattering it, the ginger ale splattering.

SARAH   BEN!

BEN SARAH! Don't leave! SARAH!

Ben tries to block the door. He moves in front of it, but Sarah sneaks out. Ben slams the door. He then reopens it and slams it closed again, in a fury.

The lights dim and, in near darkness, Ben stamps around the apartment. He lights a joint and takes a beer from the fridge and sits on the couch.

Scene 3

In near dark, Kalyan enters, dressed in a suit. His tie is loosened. He throws his suitcase and his book on the couch and sits next to Ben.

The lights fade up. The boys sit side by side, depressed.

KALYAN He asked me where I see myself in five years and I said that I would be honored to be working for him in five years. And then he said that he was disappointed to hear that because he wants employees who want *his* job in five years. He said that he wants cutthroat, hungry people and that I was disrespecting his position by not clamoring for it. So then I said I would like his job, but didn't want to presume that I could get it nor did I want to offend him by suggesting that I would be vying for his job while working for him. And then he said that was the wrong answer for two reasons: It showed dishonesty and a lack of drive. He thanked me for coming in and wished me luck with my work in *India*. Then he gave me my book, which he didn't mention once during the meeting, and made a telephone call even before I left the room.

BEN Was Ted there?

KALYAN At the beginning, yes. And it was great. Ted and Michael were joking around and including me and Ted was telling him how great I'd be. But then Michael asked him to give us some privacy. And when Ted left, the guy turned evil.

BEN That was pretty fucked up of Ted to leave you there. He can be a real asshole.

KALYAN It was like some disgusting mind trick where every answer I gave was wrong.

BEN I'm sorry man.

KALYAN The two of us. You know? Marginalized for whatever fucking unfair cosmic reason.

BEN It's like the world is trying to starve us but they keep throwing us crumbs just so we live long enough to be hungry.

KALYAN Reshma's coming over in a bit. I don't know what to say to her. She keeps calling me.

BEN Women are all assholes, in a way. And the sooner we realize that, the easier it'll be to dismiss them like the manipulative bitches that they are.

KALYAN I take it things didn't go well with Sarah?

BEN Do you want some weed?

KALYAN Maybe.

BEN Here you go. It's not that potent. Don't worry.

Kalyan takes the joint but doesn't smoke it.

KALYAN Did she come over to see your movie?

BEN Who?

KALYAN Sarah. Didn't she come over here to watch your movie?

BEN Oh, yeah, I guess she did.

KALYAN How did it go?

BEN Dude, give me that, if you're just gonna stare at it.

KALYAN Oh, sorry.

Ben takes the joint from Kalyan and takes a long hit.

BEN So, yeah, Sarah. She really dug the movie.

KALYAN Really?

BEN Yeah, it was awesome. She was so supportive.

KALYAN She didn't notice that you staged it?

BEN Well I told her about that—we have a real honest relationship —and she thought it was even more interesting because she said it was kind of like a hybrid, which was a cool way to put it. So she's probably gonna be coming over here a lot, to work on it with me, she said she wants to start doing that, to get back to doing something creative with her life after being with Ted for so long, so I hope you don't mind if she comes over here all the time and we're just hanging out privately and editing my movie together. I hope you don't mind.

KALYAN Nope. That's fine. I'm glad everything seems to be working out for you.

BEN Yeah, it's pretty great, I just think if you put your mind to something really hard you could achieve anything.

KALYAN Really? You don't think there are factors that are outside of your control?

BEN Like you not getting that job because you're from Nepal?

KALYAN Or you being independently wealthy enough to support what is essentially a hobby.

BEN No, I think if you're persistent, something good will happen. And as far as you're concerned, I think you probably had an advantage because they'd want to hire you to alleviate their guilt or meet a quota.

KALYAN You really think that?

BEN Yeah, I think race is a convenient excuse to hide behind, but it's only going to hurt you.

KALYAN Ben, that's a really hurtful thing to say.

BEN I know it feels hurtful now, but the sooner you come to terms with your identity and stuff, the happier you'll be. I'm doing you a favor.

KALYAN I can't tell what's happening right now, but I feel like I'm under attack. Can you just please tell me if that's what you're doing?

BEN Not at all. I'm in such a good place right now, with Sarah and my work, that I feel like I'm kind of in a position to be able to help my less fortunate friends.

KALYAN And I'm really happy for you that everything seems to have magically come together so quickly, but I'm feeling pretty bad about myself right now, and I would love some comforting words, not harsh advice.

BEN Shit.

KALYAN What?

BEN It's just, I don't know. Maybe this isn't the best time to ask you, brother, but I was thinking you should probably start paying some rent.

KALYAN No, Ben, this is definitely not the best time to ask me.

BEN It's just that, in the real world and stuff, things don't always happen at the best possible times.

KALYAN "The real world and stuff"? What is going on with you?

BEN No, it's just that, now that things are coming along really well for me, I need to stop acting like a selfish child. Sarah pointed out that letting you live here rent-free is actually hurting both of us, because I'm enabling you.

KALYAN Ben, I have wanted to pay you for five months, l hid the rent money in weird little spots—in your medicine cabinet, in your camera bag—and you would always deposit it back into my account.

BEN I think if you really wanted to pay me, you could've found a way. Opportunism doesn't suit you, Bunty. You've been living rent-free—

KALYAN In the apartment your father bought you! The apartment you were desperate to share with someone who would never question you. Why are you even bringing this up now?

BEN I guess because you didn't get this job and I'm just a little concerned that everything's gonna start falling on me. First it's rent, but then it's food and clothing and suddenly, you're totally dependent on me. And now, with Sarah in my life, I need to clean house a bit.

KALYAN Oh! So now you're marrying Sarah?

BEN I'm not sure what's happening with me and Sarah and I probably shouldn't even tell you this because it's none of your business and it was told to me in strict confidence but she doesn't really like Ted that much.

KALYAN She didn't say that to you.

BEN Well not those words. But she said he's so boring and only interested in dumb things like money and she was so happy to find me again. And that she's not really ready to get married and that I present a more freeing option for her.

KALYAN I don't believe that.

BEN I couldn't believe it either. It was so cool. She's so pretty. Her whole face is so unique-looking, you know?

KALYAN I don't believe you Ben.

BEN That's because you have a failure of imagination.

KALYAN So what am I supposed to do now?

BEN The thing that the world has been telling you to do at every turn. It's why your fucking girlfriend won't commit. It's why you can't get a job at that place. It's why people like me aren't going to let you freeload forever. Everything is pointing in one direction for you but you keep walking the other way.

KALYAN   And what direction is the world pointing me toward?

BEN   Going back home.

KALYAN (*stifling an explosion*)   Okay.

BEN   So what? You couldn't cut it here. It happens to millions of people every day.

KALYAN (*suppressing rage*)   Ben, I'm going to ask you to stop talking about this.

BEN   There's no shame. This is a competitive place, everyone's trying to make a quick buck and it's probably a little difficult for you to navigate—

KALYAN   Ben, please stop this right now.

BEN   And when you do go back there, you'll be welcomed with open arms and all will be forgiven. There's no reason to feel guilty—

KALYAN   *Stop telling me to go back home! Maybe I don't want to go back there!*

BEN   Why not?!

KALYAN   Because I like it here!

BEN   Then you should probably try to get your old job back!

KALYAN   What job?!

BEN   At Ray's! Or "Famous Original Ray's" or "Completely Incredible Ray's"—the pizza store!

KALYAN   I was delivering pizzas, Ben!

BEN   So what? It's honest work.

KALYAN   Honest work!? You?! Honest work!

BEN   Yeah, pizza is nothing to be ashamed of.

KALYAN   I am an intellectual! I am an important thinker!

BEN   No you're not, man. You're just another immigrant who did something of minor importance in a less than minor country.

KALYAN   Ben, I wrote a book!

BEN   Dude, no one even read your book.

KALYAN   No! You're the only one who didn't read my book.

BEN   I read your fucking book, dude. It sucked.

KALYAN   You never read it.

BEN   I did. I read it twice. It's terrible.

KALYAN   When did you read it?

BEN   When you first gave it to me. That fucking night. It's so poorly written. I don't understand economic shit maybe. But you just don't put sentences together in any satisfying way.

KALYAN   Bullshit. You didn't read it.

Ben grabs the book and flips it open.

BEN   "Part One: A Village Skirmish." You track a small village skirmish—shocker!—and the empowerment of the so-and-so clan as they collectivize and rise up.

Ben tears out this section of the book and throws it in the air. He opens to Part Two and tears that out as well.

BEN   "Part Two: Making Inroads." You document at great fucking length, at boring fucking ad infinitum the gradual inclusion of the tribesmen to the central fucking boring fucking government.

KALYAN   That's enough, Ben!

BEN (*tearing pages out*)   "Part Three: Across the Pond." You spend ten fucking pages comparing Nepal to a rising sun—wrong country by the way!

KALYAN Ben!

BEN "Part Four!—"

KALYAN BEN!!! SHUT THE FUCK UP!

Ben is quieted for a moment.

BEN I read it, I read your dumb book. I only told you I never read it because it was an easier lie than telling you I liked it.

Kalyan looks at the floor, at his torn book, distraught. Ben tries to hug him.

BEN Bunty, come here.

Kalyan storms past Ben and out the door.

The lights dim again as Ben stamps around the house. He knocks over the flowers and popcorn that he had set up for Sarah. The house is a mess.

SCENE 4

Ben smokes on the couch as the apartment buzzer sounds. Ben walks to the buzzer and presses it.

BEN Who is it?

RESHMA (*over the intercom*) Hey, it's Reshma. I was supposed to meet Kalyan, is he up there?

BEN Come on up, Reshie.

Ben buzzes the door and ambles back to the couch.

Reshma enters wearing her scrubs. She takes in the chaos of the house.

RESHMA What the hell happened in here?

BEN I was filming a horror movie and using my house as a set.

RESHMA Right. Is Kalyan here?

BEN   No, it's just me, love.

RESHMA   He's not picking up his phone.

BEN (*mock-concerned*)   Oh no!

RESHMA   He said he'd be here.

BEN   Well that doesn't make him here, Reshma! It's not like just because he said something it's magically gonna happen.

RESHMA   Whoa. Calm down.

BEN   You can't just wish for something to happen and it fucking happens. I wish Kalyan was here too! I wish the world wasn't a fucked-up string of unfair situations that I seem to be embroiled in.

RESHMA   I'm gonna go wait in his room, okay?

BEN   Okay. If you find a lamp, rub it a few times, maybe Kalyan will pop out.

RESHMA   You know, I never liked you, Ben.

BEN   Yeah, I know.

RESHMA   No, I mean I *never* liked you. Like not at one point, not for one second, since the moment I met you. I have never thought that I don't hate you.

BEN   You shouldn't use double negatives, Reshma. You're better than that.

She heads offstage to Kalyan's bedroom.

Ben looks at the scattered pages of Kalyan's book, strewn on the floor.

He begins neatening the pages, laying them together on the floor of the apartment, in the way he laid the newspaper on the floor of the classroom in his dream.

Ben delicately lies down on the papers, careful not to rustle them. Feeling nothing, he rises again, disappointed. He then composes himself and screams:

BEN Ow! Ow! Shit! Ow! I hurt myself. Reshma! I've hurt myself! I've just hurt my back!

Reshma does not come out. Ben lies back down on the papers.

BEN Reshie! I really just hurt myself and I need some help for a second. Could you come out and help me?

The door slowly opens and Reshma reenters.

BEN Hey honey, I was cleaning up all these papers for a surprise joke for Kalyan and my back just literally went out!

RESHMA Don't call me honey.

BEN Sorry, I guess I'm just a little vulnerable is all. Sorry about that. You're right. It's demeaning. But my back is really hurting.

RESHMA And what do you need me to do?

BEN If you could just stand over me . . . and help me to the couch, I'll be good. I just need to lie on the couch for a minute and then I'm good.

RESHMA Are you fucking with me?

BEN I wish! Kalyan knows all about this. I have a problem with one of my discs.

RESHMA Which one?

BEN You know, I don't even know. Isn't that crazy?

RESHMA Ben, as a doctor, I'm not sure you should be moved in this state. And, in my professional opinion, I think you're fucking with me, I just can't figure out why.

BEN No, I'm sorry, I know this is so awkward, but if you can just stand above me and help me up, I'll be good as new.

RESHMA Can we wait for Kalyan to come back?

BEN Unfortunately, we can't. It'll only take a second.

RESHMA   This is ridiculous. You're so pathetic.

BEN   I know I am.

RESHMA   It makes sense that you can't stand. You're a spineless idiot.

BEN (*a magnanimous laugh*)   You're so right. It's like my body is just manifesting what's on the inside.

RESHMA   Exactly. You'll probably be impotent in a few years.

BEN (*another laugh*)   If I'm not already! So, yeah, just stand over me, like over my face and give me your hands, it's the only way to get me up, I'm so sorry. This is so silly!

RESHMA   Okay. Fine.

Reshma is standing over Ben's legs facing him and offering her hands.

BEN   It's actually easier if you come higher up. Like over my face.

Reshma sighs and walks up to stand over Ben's face.

BEN   And if you could just turn around.

RESHMA   Ben, I don't really have time for this.

Reshma turns around, straddling Ben's face in the right way. She looks at the floor, noticing Kalyan's book for the first time.

RESHMA   What is that?

BEN   What's what?

RESHMA   This is Kalyan's book.

BEN   Is it?

Suddenly, and with great force, Ben grabs her ankles.

RESHMA   OW! What the fuck are you doing?

BEN   Don't move! Just don't move!

RESHMA   Ben! Get the fuck off of me.

He is squeezing her ankles tightly and she falls over, her head between his legs.

BEN   Stop yelling! Just stop yelling!

Suddenly, the door swings open and Kalyan enters.

KALYAN   What the fuck are you doing?

Kalyan tears Reshma out of Ben's ankle-grip. Ben perks up.

BEN   Hey, Bunty!

Kalyan punches Ben in the face.

BEN   Ach!!

KALYAN   What are you doing to her? What was he doing to you?

RESHMA   You fucking asshole! You selfish fucking prick asshole!

Reshma tries to attack Ben, but Kalyan holds her back.

KALYAN   Resh! Get off him!

Kalyan forces Reshma to sit on the couch.

KALYAN   Are you hurt?

RESHMA   You motherfucking asshole!!

Reshma lunges at Ben, but Kalyan, with force, sits her down on the couch.

KALYAN   HEY! ARE YOU HURT?

RESHMA   No.

KALYAN   Good. Then sit down.

She complies. Ben writhes on the floor.

BEN   Ow . . . Bunty . . .

KALYAN   What the fuck is wrong with you?

Ben picks up some of the pages of Kalyan's book that he's lying on.

BEN   I'm sorry, man. I couldn't find any newspaper.

KALYAN   I just went to the ATM.

Kalyan pulls out an envelope and throws wads of bills at Ben.

KALYAN   April! (*another wad*)   May! (*another*)   June! (*and another*)   July! (*and finally*)   August!

Ben is lying in the pool of cash.

KALYAN   Now I'm all paid up. You can give this to your father.

BEN   Nah, I'll probably just hang on to it.

KALYAN   Then you're a shitty son.

Kalyan takes Reshma.

KALYAN   Let's go.

He takes her out of the apartment. Ben is on the floor, dazed.

The lights shift slightly, to indicate a passage of time.

SCENE 5

Ben is asleep on the floor, in the same spot we left him.

The door opens and Ted enters, surveying the disastrous scene and Ben, passed out.

TED   Ben. Hey, you okay, buddy?

Teddy walks over to Ben and cradles his head. Ben groggily wakes up, speaks in a uniquely innocent tone:

BEN   Teddy.

TED   Hey man.

BEN   I think I've been unconscious for a while. Kalyan punched me.

TED   Yeah, I know.

BEN   What day is it?

TED   It's the same day.

BEN   Oh.

TED   That was about ten minutes ago. He called me and Sarah to come check on you.

BEN   That was nice of him.

TED   Yeah. Sarah's downstairs, she's waiting in the car.

BEN   Oh. (*pause*) You guys have a car?

TED   We use her mother's.

BEN   Oh, how nice.

TED   Yeah, we keep it at a garage around the corner.

BEN (*sweet*)   That sounds like a nice arrangement.

TED   It's not too bad. It's good for day trips.

They chuckle together sweetly.

BEN   And Sarah's not scared to drive in the city?

TED   No, she's great. She's aggressive.

BEN   Hmm. I would have thought she'd be scared.

Sarah enters the apartment.

BEN   Hey Sarah, I was unconscious for a few minutes. Kalyan punched me.

SARAH   I know.

BEN   I'll probably be fine. It doesn't feel concussed or anything.

SARAH   Ben, I came over to tell you something. But before I do, I want you to know that I'm not sure you deserve to hear what I'm about to tell you.

BEN   Okay.

SARAH   Good. Earlier, you asked me if I remembered you doing anything interesting in school. I remembered something. And I want to tell it to you.

BEN   Okay.

SARAH   And even though I don't know if you deserve to hear this, I think the world will be a better place if you do.

BEN   Okay.

SARAH   Do you remember when Inga Lushenko moved to Princeton Junction?

BEN   Not really.

SARAH   Yes you do. Ted, you remember Inga Lushenko, right?

TED   Vaguely. I don't think I really knew her though.

SARAH   We all had gym together.

TED   Well you don't really *talk* to anyone in gym.

SARAH   You know who she is. She was from Ukraine and some douche bag started a rumor that she was affected by Chernobyl or something. And that she was gonna grow like three arms from the radiation poisoning. Do you remember that, Ben?

BEN   I don't know.

TED   Right! Everyone thought she had like deadly radiation that was really contagious. Which I don't think is actually true.

SARAH   Of course it's not true, you idiot.

TED   Well she was a little weird-looking.

SARAH   She had a gap in her teeth like every other ten-year-old. And so, anyway, no one would go near her. For months, everyone avoided Inga Lushenko, thinking they'd become infected by her "Chernobyl syndrome." Until you, Ben, did the craziest thing.

BEN I feel like I'm not going to be proud of what you're about to say.

SARAH Well, you should be. At recess, some girls were making fun of her and pretending to like quarantine her on the playground, under the jungle gym. And you stripped your clothes off—you must have been like ten years old—

BEN I was eleven.

SARAH Eleven. So you do remember. You were just in your little tighty whities and you ran up to Inga and tackled her. And you kind of started humping her.

TED Yes! I do remember that! It was hysterical.

SARAH But the brilliance of it was that it looked like you were just making fun of her, or torturing her like everyone else. But that's not what you were doing, was it?

BEN I don't know.

SARAH You were saving her.

BEN They suspended me from recess for six weeks.

SARAH But after you did that, something changed. You weren't infected with radiation and suddenly she wasn't scary anymore. She suddenly became normal but no one could figure out exactly why.

TED It was a stealth move.

SARAH And I remember that after they pulled you off of her and led you back into the school, she was just lying on the playground. And I thought she would be hysterically crying. But she was just laying there on the ground smiling to herself. And I don't think I had ever seen Inga smile. And I knew what you had done for her. I was ten years old and I think, for the first time, I learned what sacrifice was.

Ben chokes up. He covers his whole face with his hands.

SARAH   And I work with the toughest kids in this city and I see things that seem like little acts of heroism every day. But they're not little. Because at ten years old, those are the things you remember forever. And I bet Inga Lushenko probably thinks of you every day Ben. Maybe in a way that she doesn't even realize. But whenever she thinks the world is awful and that people are evil and uncaring, she'll remember in the way back of her mind that some crazy kid took off his clothes on the playground and tackled her, letting everyone else know that she was safe to touch. Do you remember that, Ben?

Ben is silent.

TED   Ben?

He doesn't move.

SARAH   That was a nice memory for me.

TED   Hey, Ben. Do you remember that?

Ben slowly lowers his hands and looks up.

Blackout.